Higher Education Outside of the Academy

Jeffrey A. Cantor

ASHE-ERIC Higher Education Report Volume 27, Number 7
Adrianna J. Kezar, Series Editor

Prepared and published by

JOSSEY-BASS
A Wiley Company
San Francisco

In cooperation with

ERIC Clearinghouse on Higher Education
The George Washington University
URL: www.eriche.org

Association for the Study
of Higher Education
URL: www.tiger.coe.missouri.edu/~ashe

Graduate School of Education and Human Development
The George Washington University
URL: www.gwu.edu

Higher Education Outside of the Academy
Jeffrey A. Cantor (au.)
ASHE-ERIC Higher Education Report Volume 27, Number 7
Adrianna J. Kezar, Series Editor

This publication was prepared partially with funding from the
Office of Educational Research and Improvement, U.S.
Department of Education, under contract no. ED-99-00-0036.
The opinions expressed in this report do not necessarily re-
flect the positions or policies of OERI or the Department.

ISSN 0884-0040   ISBN 0-7879-5696-1

The ASHE-ERIC Higher Education Report is part of the
Jossey-Bass Higher and Adult Education Series and is pub-
lished eight times a year by Jossey-Bass, 350 Sansome Street,
San Francisco, California 94104-1342.

For subscription information, see the Back Issue/
Subscription Order Form in the back of this journal.

Prospective authors are strongly encouraged to contact
Adrianna Kezar, Director, ERIC Clearinghouse on Higher
Education, at (202) 296-2597 ext. 14 or akezar@eric-he-edu.

Visit the Jossey-Bass Web site at www.josseybass.com.

Printed in the United States of America on acid-free recycled
paper containing 100 percent recovered waste paper, of
which at least 20 percent is postconsumer waste.

EXECUTIVE SUMMARY

In an era when business recognizes that its human resources are the single most important ingredient for corporate success, training has become an invaluable enterprise. American industry recognizes that the skills of workers at all levels will continue to need to improve in response to rapid technological changes. At the same time, what has come to be recognized as the classic model of the university is changing as a result of industry's new and emerging needs for knowledge, constant technological innovation, education's place in the economy, and diminishing funding (Skilbeck & Connell, 1996). This report addresses joint initiatives and programs from higher education and business and industry from outside the academy.

How Have Training and Human Resource Development for Business and Industry Grown as a Form of Higher Education?

The growth of higher education outside the academy has involved and affected three entities: the college or university itself, the corporate or business community, and the community at large. This report looks at each entity and its relationship with the other two. Six distinct but interrelated activities underpin this movement:

- The growth of training and human resource development as delivered by a firm for its employees and customers as a form of higher education
- The growth of the corporate university—training and human resource development delivered by a company for its employees and customers, often in cooperation and partnership with colleges and universities
- Colleges' and universities' use of computer-based technologies to deliver instruction to their students
- College-developed training delivered on site to local businesses and industries
- The growth and proliferation of private and for-profit institutions of higher education
- An increasing presence of nontraditional nonprofit community-based organizations providing education and training in competition with traditional institutions of higher education

Both education and training have a role to play in meeting the mission and objectives of twenty-first century colleges and universities.

How Have Private and Nontraditional Institutions of Higher Education Grown?

In addition to the many businesses that provide training for their employees, the 1990s witnessed a growth in the number of private and proprietary and nonprofit institutions offering college-level education to a growing number of nontraditional students (McCandless, 1998). Hence, these institutions have identified significant niche markets as a result of college students' changing demographics and demands. The traditional university is no longer without competition for a student body. A host of learning organizations, including museums, profit-making organizations, and publishers, and the new technology have converged to bring about a global learning community offering students a plethora of international educational opportunities.

How Have Colleges Developed and Delivered Training to Local Business and Industry as a Source of Additional Revenue?

The search for alternative sources of funding for the academy has caused both administrators and faculty to rethink their relationships with their corporate neighbors (Aronowitz, 1998). Higher education's response to the challenges of external study has taken two predominant forms. One is partnerships with business and industry to provide contract training to meet specific needs of the workplace. The second is the development of mechanisms to recognize education and training provided by organizations external to the traditional academy. This monograph looks at how colleges and business have combined to solve mutual problems of educating a citizenry and a workforce. It looks at programmatic partnerships in areas where workers are in high demand, as well as the processes and conventions that have evolved in the academy in order to recognize industry or corporate training as part of the academic degree program.

How and Why Has the Concept of the Corporate University Grown?

The corporate university is an institution developed by business and industry to meet businesses' changing needs created by a global economy and increased competition. At the time of Nash and Hawthorne's work about employer-sponsored instruction (1987), about 400 firms had initiated and developed corporate universities to educate and train employees. The impetus for the corporate university was to obtain quality educational services at competitive prices to maintain a skilled workforce and to create a learning organization to compete in a global economy (Meister, 1998b).

Based on this review of the literature, a model for proactive cooperation between the academy and external organizations and constituencies emerges. Its focus is on making decisions about when to compete with other organizations providing education and training in the community and how to cooperate with other community-based constituents in providing education and training outside the academy.

CONTENTS

FOREWORD

The increased development of training and education outside traditional higher education has captured the imagination of the press and the public. Yet the majority of individuals in the academy continue their work of scholarship, teaching, and service with little concern about this emerging trend. Should academics be concerned? Jeffrey A. Cantor, dean of extended studies and workforce education at Norwalk Community College, describes why he thinks the academy should attend to this trend. This thoughtful discussion helps educators and the public to understand the environmental forces creating the development of higher education outside the academy and the role higher education should play in this new marketplace.

Several forces establish context for this trend toward education outside traditional institutions, including the significant growth in dollars spent on development of employees by corporations. To meet this growing demand, proprietary schools, on-line educators, and corporate universities have grown to fill this market niche. Motorola, American Express, Cigna, Oracle Corp., and others have changed the face of workforce development. In addition, over the last 20 years, older students have increasingly become a market within postsecondary education. This population faces constraints on time and flexibility that are not being addressed by traditional higher education. Moreover, the economy has changed such that lifelong learning is necessary in order to be competitive as an employee.

After two decades of growth outside the academy, institutions of higher learning have begun to develop models to respond, including professional studies schools and consortial relationships between traditional higher education and corporate universities. The major impetus for this response has been the competition for students who have greater options, particularly on-line options such as the Open University of the United States or the University of Phoenix.

The genius of this monograph is its restraint on overgeneralizing or prophesying the end of the academy if it does not respond to the changing environment. Instead, Cantor focuses on opportunities to capitalize on these new markets. Yet the best way to respond is by being informed, using the best practices we know about how to develop proactive, cooperative partnerships between the academy and external organizations. Many institutions are running toward opportunity without the guidance and wisdom gained through earlier partnerships. This monograph fills this gap in our knowledge by showcasing model partnerships and research on these efforts.

Some of the principles learned from early partnerships include the need for academic institutions to focus on their strengths—content and expertise—and partner with other organizations that provide technological expertise and infrastructure or venture capital. Higher education institutions need to become more aware of the strengths they can bring to partnerships by conducting an audit of their institution to assess their strengths for partnerships. Partnerships must include dialogue about values. Corporations often have very different values from the academy, and these different value systems must be negotiated up front to develop a successful partnership. Ownership of intellectual capital is another critical element to clarify. This monograph delineates these and many other important principles. As Cantor states in the conclusion, "Successful colleges and universities of tomorrow will be able to enter into partnerships and joint ventures that maximize their resources and attract the kinds of resources and capabilities from outside that bring new opportunities for the student body and faculty." It is hoped that this monograph will help you create successful joint ventures!

Several other ASHE-ERIC monographs will assist in the development of these partnerships, among them *The Virtual Campus: Technology and Reform in Higher Education* by Gerald Van Dusen, which examines the way that traditional higher education can embrace the promise of technology; *Experiential Learning in Higher Education: Linking Classroom and Community,* Cantor's earlier monograph, which examines partnerships between corporations and schools from the perspective of student learning; and *Prices, Productivity, and Investment: Assessing Financial Strategies in Higher Education* by Edward St. John, which explores the ways partnerships might help foster greater financial health for institutions. Developing partnerships, embracing technology, focusing on students and institutional mission, and maintaining sound financial practices are all important principles for colleges and universities in the twenty-first century.

Adrianna J. Kezar
Series Editor

ACKNOWLEDGMENTS

A work of this magnitude requires able assistance from skilled and knowledgeable people. To these ends, I thank my partner and wife Ruth for her assistance with this project. Without Ruth I could not have achieved a fraction of what I have been able to accomplish in my academic career or personal life.

I also thank my mentor and employer, William H. Schwab, president of Norwalk Community College, and my colleague, Sally Bolster, for their critical reviews of the manuscript.

INTRODUCTION AND OVERVIEW

This report is about the growth and proliferation of higher education delivered outside the academy. It describes the extent to which corporate America and other organizations and institutions have entered the business of providing formal higher and adult education to their constituents and customers. It analyzes the manner and extent to which traditional academic institutions have responded to this competition and challenge, and to the needs of a changing student body. Following an earlier report (Nash & Hawthorne, 1987) on corporate higher education, it illustrates the tremendous growth in interest and activity since that report was published.

The growth of higher education outside the academy has involved and affected three entities: the college or university itself, the corporate or business community, and the community at large. This report looks at each entity and its relationship with the other two. Six distinct but interrelated activities underpin this movement:

- *The growth of training and human resource development as delivered by a firm for its employees and customers as a form of higher education.* Corporate offerings range from technical skills to customer services. The business community needs to invest in its workforce to stay competitive in a global economy.
- *The growth of the corporate university—training and human resource development delivered by a company for its employees and customers, often in cooperation and partnership with colleges and universities.* Organizations from Motorola Corp. to local credit unions are creating corporate universities to educate and train workers. The business community recognizes the need to offer its workforce access to academic credits and degrees as part of training and development.
- *Colleges' and universities' use of computer-based technologies to deliver instruction to their students.* Our traditional student body is changing. As a result of increasing demands on time and financial resources, students are demanding access to college study via the Internet. Of particular interest are the international implications of increased use of the Internet for studies outside the academy.
- *College-developed training delivered on site to local businesses and industries.* Colleges have recognized the

The business community needs to invest in its workforce to stay competitive in a global economy.

market created by business and industry for quality training. Colleges and universities, both public and private, are now embracing this market to generate monies to supplement diminishing tax revenues and endowments. This activity has long been part of most colleges' missions. International borders are dissolving as the Internet makes it possible to study abroad without leaving home.

- *The growth and proliferation of private and for-profit institutions of higher education.* As the market for corporate training increases, proprietary institutions flourish. Kaplan Learning Centers, DeVry Inc., and ITT Technical Institutes are but a few of the growing number of firms. And as students continue to seek quick-response technical training and Internet-based training, private higher education is growing rapidly as well.
- *An increasing presence of nontraditional nonprofit community-based organizations providing education and training in competition with traditional institutions of higher education,* including the Corporation for Public Broadcasting and the American Red Cross. Likewise, the number of alternate venues for accessing college-level education is growing as a result of these various forces.

This monograph was written during what history will undoubtedly refer to as the dawn of the information age. Electronic and digital communications form the backbone and infrastructure of most business and personal communication systems today. Both the way in which people communicate and the speed at which business and life itself move have changed dramatically. While the state of the art in communications and information technology has expanded exponentially, this technology is only beginning to affect higher education and the human resource development professions.

Underlying Assumptions and Limitations of This Report
This report was commissioned as a follow-up to an earlier report on higher education outside the academy (Nash & Hawthorne, 1987), which discussed college practices and education of the workforce during the 1980s. Much has changed since that time.

Not all in the academic community embrace wholeheartedly the magnitude of growth in business-academic partnerships, and it is widely agreed that academic institutions should strive to remain autonomous in formulating curricula and academic policy. But as the state of the world's economic and political competitiveness has become more dynamic and visible, higher education has been called on to respond in kind. This response has manifested itself in many different and diverse ways, including formation of significant partnerships for program delivery and technology development. Yet, as Slaughter (1998) suggests, in some regards "the economic functions of higher education have moved to the foreground, the educational functions to the background" (p. 209).

The approach to this work is strictly from the standpoint of describing issues surrounding the offer and delivery of programs outside the academy in cooperation with business and industry. It illustrates the growth in these areas since Nash and Hawthorne's work in the late 1980s. The literature reviewed for this report focuses on colleges' and universities' practices in educating the workforce; the databases searched include those of the Educational Resources Information Center as well as some from business and commerce. Throughout, we should not lose sight of the fact that "the media attention given to the relatively few multi-million dollar research agreements between a handful of elite academic institutions and corporations has masked other significant contributions that academic institutions have made to the economy, particularly through training the workforce" (Fairweather, 1990, p. 40).

Reasons for the Growth of Higher Education Delivered Outside the Academy

The literature identifies several issues as predominant forces affecting a movement of nontraditional institutions' sponsoring and offering formalized education and training, including the kinds of credentials that are now being recognized as benchmarks of competency for the purposes of preparing workers and addressing business leaders' concerns about the availability of appropriate and timely educational services for their workers. Students themselves express concerns about the ability of traditional colleges and universities to respond to their needs with appropriate offerings and services.

Business leaders' concerns

In an era when business now recognizes that its human resources are the single most important ingredient for successful corporate growth, training and higher education have become an invaluable investment in business development. This work explores several issues facing American businesses: cost of and expenditures for human resource development, levels of participation, providers of training and educational opportunities, curricula, methods of instruction, organization for training, and evaluation.

Students' concerns

Students' concerns have driven the movement toward higher education outside the traditional academy as well. The average age of students in undergraduate (and graduate) programs has risen in recent years. Many students today seek alternatives to traditional classroom (Levine, 1998).

The constraints placed on students arising from family obligations and work cause them to seek out alternatives to higher education that maximize scarce time resources. Students seek out distance learning technologies, including Web-based courses, televised courses, and courses given at the workplace. Computer technology is quickly becoming the popular medium of choice. These issues are also explored in this monograph.

Degree versus industry certification

More than half of all jobs created between 1984 and 2005 will require post–high school education. "The implication for higher education is that an A.A., B.A., and even an M.A. [are] now viewed by employers as merely preparing students for a lifetime of education and training" (American Society for Training and Development, 1998, p. 2). These forms of post-secondary education and training are rapidly changing. Today, the issue of industry-based, industry-developed certification is surfacing. The concept of having a student demonstrate competency in a specific set of occupational skills by passing a certification exam is quickly becoming popular. Examples include information technology certifications such as Microsoft's MCSE (Microsoft Certified Systems Engineer) and Cisco Systems CNA (Certified Network Associate). Many colleges, such as Old Dominion University, package courses around these certifications, and some recognize the certificate for college credit. Higher education institutions are being forced to address certifications in their academic programs, and many schools are adopting industry programs such as those offered by Oracle Corporation (the Oracle Academic Initiative) and Novell Corporation. These certification programs have also caused the growth of higher education outside the traditional academy.

The data clearly indicate that companies believe higher education has room for improvement when it comes to communicating what they can do for corporations and how well they perform in partnerships (American Society for Training and Development, 1998, p. 3). Academics, however, do not fully accept the arguments of the business world that the traditional academy is slow and unresponsive (Aronowitz, 1998). This monograph explores the kinds of initiatives undertaken by the academy to meet business needs internal and external to the academy. The ultimate question to be addressed is the long-range impact on higher education if this trend continues.

The convergence of these various forces has caused a revolution of sorts in higher education. Some colleges and universities have essentially ignored the competition and calls for change, while others have responded in kind. Should colleges strive to meet the competition, thus reacting as businesses rather than conservatories of knowledge? Will the traditional academy survive both the economic and technological upheavals of this and the next decade? Attempts to answer these questions form the focal point for this monograph.

Overview of the Monograph
Why have American business and industry focused increased attention on human resource development? Present labor shortages necessitate an investment in initial and continuing training. In addition, American industry recognizes that the skills of workers at all levels will continue to increase in response to rapid technological changes (Watson, 1995), while, according to Meister (1998a), knowledge has an increasingly shortened shelf life, exacerbated by rapid technological changes. Both situations fuel the growth of a firm's investment in educating its employees.

On the other side of the table is the increase in corporate development of higher education alternatives as a result of business and industry's disappointment with the responsiveness of traditional higher education to its need for workers. Corporate concerns include poor responsiveness on the part of academe—which is slow to make changes in curriculum and instructional delivery systems to meet corporate needs—and/or poor customer orientation. "Community colleges and universities are critical resources in gaining competitive advantage in the knowledge age—especially for technology companies. But since the interweaving of markets and academics is a recent phenomenon, schools—notably universities—have been slow to change from a vendor to consultant relationship" (American Society for Training and Development, 1998, p. 1).

Further,

> *This shortened shelf life of knowledge, coupled with the fast pace of technological change, is fueling the growth of investment in employee education. Businesses must constantly upgrade the skill and competency levels of knowledge workers to remain competitive. To meet this challenge, corporations are increasingly developing joint degree programs with institutions of higher education. . . .*
>
> *These degrees are primarily at the graduate level in business administration, computer science, engineering, and finance. The driver for this interest in offering accredited learning programs is the desire to grant portable credentials as part of the corporate training program.* (Meister, 1998a, p. 3)

How much is actually spent? According to the American Society for Training and Development, business and industry spent $55.3 billion on education and training in 1995 (Bassi & Van Buren, 1998). These figures represent 1.4 to 1.8 percent of an average surveyed firm's payroll nationally. Larger firms invest 3 percent of their personnel dollars in training, whereas small companies invest between 5 to 7 percent to keep employees' skills on the cutting edge and remain competitive (Watson, 1995). A typical firm with 50 or more employees spent an average of $504 per employee on training. These figures represent a significant increase over the $30 billion spent on education and training in 1984 (Nash & Hawthorne, 1987).

Increasingly, American industry is seeking out colleges and universities to provide the training and development support it needs rather than increasing in-house staff (Ouellete, 1998), and colleges are embracing these relationships (Evelyn, 1999). Conservatively, colleges and universities provide 20 to 30 percent of the education and training for business and industry (National Alliance of Business, 1997). This training spans the gamut from basic and technical skills to managerial skills and graduate education. What kinds of industries train their workers, and in what proportions do they provide their own training?

According to *Training & Development's* "1998 ASTD State of the Industry Report," 69 percent of all firms surveyed provided some type of training for workers (Bassi & Van Buren, 1998). By industry segment, 82 percent of health care firms surveyed provided worker in-service training, compared with 71 percent of high-tech firms, 68 percent of light manufacturing firms, 66 percent of business service firms, and 62 percent of customer services firms.

Areas of instruction provided in such education and training courses, according to the same survey, included management and supervision skills (93 percent), computer literacy and applications (91 percent), job-specific technical skills (88 percent), occupational safety (84 percent), teamwork (77 percent), quality assurance and best practices (76 percent), and executive development (63 percent).

The survey found that 27.3 percent of U.S. firms' training budgets goes to acquiring training from outside the firm itself. Sources for such training, according to the survey, are independent firms (73 percent), consultants (68 percent), community colleges (42 percent), and other educational institutions (48 percent). In fact, numerous businesses offer courses in cooperation with colleges and universities that lead to associate, baccalaureate, and master's degrees.

What are the effects of technology on the delivery of training programs? Eighteen percent of corporate-sponsored training is now delivered using technology—over the Internet, by satellite, or with desktop teleconferencing (National Alliance of Business, 1997). The advent and increasing popularity of computers and the Internet have opened up new market opportunities for traditional and nontraditional higher education institutions wishing to serve local business and industry. "The Proliferation of Corporate Education and Training" discusses these developments.

"The Privatization of Higher Education" discusses the proliferation of private and for-profit ventures in the delivery of higher education services. Motivated in part by the growth of information technology and acceptance of the computer for processing information and interacting with the world, today's students are now demanding "just-in-time" education and training when and where they choose (McCandless, 1998). For-profit ventures comprising educators and computer scientists have stepped to the forefront to meet this demand.

This section discusses the growth of private and proprietary institutions of higher education, including the University of Phoenix and DeVry Institutes. Not all of higher education follows the traditional public or private university format. The last two decades have witnessed a plethora of profit-making organizations such as Harcourt, Inc., granting degrees (Levine & Cureton, 1998), and many enterprises such as ITT Technical Institutes and DeVry Institutes have become established in the higher education market (Stamps, 1998). DeVry Institutes has grown to one of the largest private ventures offering technical higher education courses.

As a result of this movement, traditional higher education institutions are becoming concerned that private industry is becoming a formidable competitor where competition previously did not exist. "The Privatization of Higher Education" also explores the ways that traditional institutions such as New York University have created for-profit ventures to capture segments of the professional adult student market. New York University in October 1998 announced the development of a for-profit subsidiary that will develop and sell specialized on-line courses. This venture is aimed at marketing to other colleges, corporate training centers, and students who prefer to take higher education courses at home or in the office (Arenson, 1998). This venture follows the successes of the University of Phoenix, which has grown to 111 "campuses" across the western United States.

Universities and colleges, community and special interest groups have geared up to offer higher education courses and degrees over the Internet. The proliferation of Web- and computer-based courses has caused traditional academic institutions to rethink their policies for scheduling and instructional delivery. Many institutions have ventured into partnerships with software vendors and proprietary firms to offer on-line instruction. Rio Hondo College and New York University, for example, have developed "virtual" colleges to serve their constituencies. Commercial ventures have developed the Web-based infrastructure to assist colleges with these efforts. "The rapid growth and proliferation of information technologies are breaking down the walls separating markets, institutions, and society" (American Society for Training and Development, 1998, p. 1).

Once considered a bastion of stability, if not tranquillity, higher education during the 1990s witnessed significant turbulence and change. Much of this turbulence has resulted from the economic and technological conditions of this age. The maturation of the information age and the resulting effects on the economy have resulted in tremendous pressures placed on higher education for quick responses to changing skills needed for the next generation of educated and trained workers. Although schools "have been slow to change from a vendor to consultant relationship" (American Society for Training and Development, 1998, p. 1), both employers and workers have come to the realization that college degrees without the requisite skills for particular jobs and occupations are of limited value. "Academe's Response" discusses and analyzes the literature surrounding this movement toward college-business-community partnerships and implications for traditional higher education institutions. Meister (1998b) argues that these educational partnerships parallel the organizational streamlining and reengineering of corporate America, where training activities are being brought more closely in line with corporate goals. A significant movement since Nash and Hawthorne's publication has been the formation of such partnerships between corporate America and institutions of higher education to train workers.

What are some configurations of partnerships? In recent years, more emphasis has been directed to industry-sanctioned certifications and similar benchmarks of competency (Perez & Copenhaver, 1998). In the forefront of

The maturation of the information age and the resulting effects on the economy have resulted in tremendous pressures placed on higher education for quick responses to changing skills needed for the next generation of educated and trained workers.

this movement have been partnerships between information technology firms and colleges to facilitate training in the software and computer fields.

"Academe's Response" analyzes the literature surrounding the movement toward partnerships and discusses implications for the academy. "Corporate partnerships with traditional universities succeed when both parties think carefully about what is expected from the other—and about how to bridge the very real differences in culture between the corporate and academic worlds" (Meister, 1998a, p. 3). Ouellette (1998) underscores some of these concerns with traditional university programs: "Companies are finding that generic courses may not deliver the best punch for their dollars. So the latest trend is to negotiate outsourcing contracts in which a university provides courses and technical degrees customized for a particular business" (p. 20). Significant partnerships between corporate America and the academy discussed in this section include those promoted by information technology firms such as Cisco Systems, Microsoft, Oracle Corporation, and Novell Corporation.

"Academe's Response" also discusses college/university contract training, continuing education, and extended studies and how they have enabled colleges to meet the demands of business and thus retain their share of the corporate education and training market, and some organizational issues. "What was once the hidden curriculum—the subordination of higher education to the needs of capital—has become an open, frank policy of public and private education" (Aronowitz, 1998, p. 33). The need to fund colleges and universities has been a prime motivator toward higher education's willingness to recognize the needs of business and industry.

The section also discusses other mechanisms and processes developed by the academic establishment to bridge academe and industry, such as the American Council on Education's processes for recognition of industry education and training for academic credit. A 1997 survey by Quality Dynamics found that many corporate universities plan to offer A.S., B.S., and graduate degrees in subjects ranging from business management to manufacturing management to health care (Sammarco, 1997). Employers see these degrees as portable credentials for their employees. In fact, the Virginia Community College

System has developed an associate degree in technical studies to permit its 23 member colleges to rapidly respond to businesses' needs by offering a degree "shell" that can be customized and tailored with major technical courses to meet a particular industry's needs.

Long-term synergistic and mutually beneficial partnerships are being formed as universities move down from their ivory towers to build alliances with corporate America. Historically, universities have relied on corporations to provide them with funds and, more importantly, a ready market for their open enrollment executive education courses. What is changing now is the number and depth of corporate/college alliances, which are becoming much more multifaceted and strategic. (Meister, 1998a, p. 3)

The American Council on Education's College Credit Recommendation Service provides a standard for college or university recognition of business and industry training that regional accrediting agencies recognize and respect. Therefore, businesses and industries can better provide students of local colleges and schools opportunities for college credit and ultimately a degree (Kurschner, 1997).

A significant amount of military education and training occurs annually, much of it at a level that merits college credit. Through DANTES, service people and their dependents can pursue higher education while on active duty and without disruption because of a change in duty stations (Golfin & Curtin, 1998). "Academe's Response" looks at several aspects of this movement in higher education.

Organizations such as the Corporation for Public Broadcasting have also ventured into nontraditional higher education, offering televised courses students can take for college credit. Students who are interested in earning college credit for a course offered through the televised satellite service can register for college credit through a participating college or university in their state or region. In Connecticut, for instance, a student can register through Charter Oak College.

Many hospitals and other health care institutions offer education and training for their employees as well as for members of the community. Through partnerships and affiliation with a local college or university, students can earn college credit. Continuing medical education is another variation of extended learning often offered in cooperation with hospitals and health care organizations. Colleges have become more sensitive to the needs of these organizations and their constituencies and have developed partnerships to support these community needs.

Finally, the section looks at the roles and reactions of the various accrediting agencies with respect to partnerships between higher education and nontraditional providers of college courses.

Companies of all kinds are transforming into "learning organizations." One major component of a learning organization is increasingly referred to as the "corporate university." Nash and Hawthorne (1987) discussed and described the genesis of corporate universities and defined the corporate university as a degree-granting institution established by an entity whose major mission is something other than education. "Corporate universities aren't a place, but a concept for organized learning that's designed to perpetuate the organization" (Slavenski, cited in Bachler, 1997b). Since Nash and Hawthorne's report, the corporate university movement has grown tenfold. According to the National Alliance of Business (1997), more than 1,200 corporate universities are currently in existence, up from 400 in the late 1980s. "The Corporate Response" explores why corporate America has invested so heavily in the corporate university and discusses the elements of a corporate university and the types of training provided for employees.

Based on this review of the literature, "Developing a Sustaining Model for Partnerships" discusses a model for proactive cooperation between the academy and external organizations and constituencies. Once the issues have been identified, the traditional academy should be able to compete on a level playing field. "Training departments will find new ways to deliver services to cope with the demand for quality instruction, [including] structures to support networks of internal and external providers" (Bassi, Cheney, & Van Buren, 1997, p. 47). Let us hope the academy does as well.

THE PROLIFERATION OF CORPORATE EDUCATION AND TRAINING IN THE WORKPLACE

This section highlights education and training programs provided by business and industry to employees. While these programs are intended primarily to provide work skills necessary to accomplish jobs and tasks associated with producing goods and services rather than to educate workers as well-rounded and erudite members of society, the enterprise of education and training in the corporation has become a major segment of higher education outside the traditional academy. "Today, it's becoming increasingly common to see business working hand in hand with education to teach, equip and prepare students to enter and succeed in the workplace" (C. Taylor, 1999, p. 4). The definition of higher education is changing as the workplace becomes more complex and entrepreneurs need to invest more heavily in educating workers.

Expenditures for Human Resource Development

Education and training of corporate employees represents the majority of adult education conducted outside of academic institutions (Eurich, 1990). As business leaders recognize the need to invest in training and development of workers, corporate spending for training is growing (Bassi, Cheney, & Lewis, 1998; Hoy, 1998). As discussed herein, corporate America has come to realize that the single most important resource available to a firm is its human resources—its people. Whether the firm provides a service or manufactures a product, the performance of workers becomes the factor determining productivity and ultimately the firm's competitive edge (Bassi & Cheney, 1997). To these ends, most firms today recognize the value of being a "learning organization," the new terminology for a workforce engaged in continual learning, formal and informal (Bassi & Van Buren, 1999). Many firms have developed internal organizations to support in-house training. Many believe that they must control the delivery of these programs to ensure that requirements for content and quality are met. Others believe that through outsourcing and partnerships with professional training organizations, the requirements can be met cost-effectively outside their firms (Bassi & Cheney, 1997; Eurich, 1990).

Certainly, colleges and universities have made their presence known in their communities, as witnessed by the phenomenal growth in continuing education programs.

In many colleges and universities, adult student credit-free enrollments now count for nearly half of all college enrollments (Gose, 1999).

Yet business and industry–sponsored training continues to grow in magnitude, presenting additional opportunities and challenges to traditional higher education (Bosley, 1995). Should higher education offer its services more aggressively or simply coexist as training providers with separate and different programs? The answer rests in "enlightened self-interest" (Wenrich, 1999) by knowing and understanding what kinds of training business and industry provide internally and how we as educators can be in the best position to judge where partnerships and cooperative ventures make sense. This section gives an overview of training provided by business and industry, including:

- Levels of participation in employer-sponsored training by types of firms
- Prominent areas of training and education in industry
- External providers of training and education to firms
- Predominant methods of instruction
- Organization for training within the corporation

Through an analysis of empirical data, we can better understand the magnitude of expenditures American business dedicates to training employees. Empirical data on business-sponsored training can be useful to college administrators and faculty alike in planning for future educational programming, and in developing articulation agreements with businesses in areas where cooperative ventures appear appropriate. Our nation's 1,250 two-year colleges are increasingly aligning with their local businesses (the future employers of their students) to guide the college on "everything from the general skills they'd like to see in the graduates to specific curriculum content" (Evelyn, 1999, p. 6). Gose (1999) discusses the issues related to generating new sources of operating revenue for colleges.

The most recent data available at the time this report was written are found in the 1995 data set produced by the U.S. Bureau of Labor Statistics (BLS) and supplemented by several training industry studies, including two studies conducted by the American Society for Training and Development. The first, the 1997 Human Performance

Practices Survey covering data for calendar year 1996, was conducted in cooperation with Times-Mirror Training Group, Development Dimensions International, the Forum Corporation, and the U.S. Department of Labor and was reported in "1998 ASTD State of the Industry Report" (Bassi & Van Buren, 1998). A second similar survey was conducted in 1998 for calendar year 1997 (Bassi & Van Buren, 1999). It includes data from 85 organizations that participated in the previous year's study. For the 1997 survey, a random sample of U.S. firms with 50 or more employees was drawn from the industry categories of high technology; finance, insurance, and real estate (FIRE); business services; heavy manufacturing; extraction and construction; light manufacturing; transportation, communications, and public utilities (TCPU); and health care and customer service. Data from a survey by the Saratoga Institute (National Alliance of Business, 1997) are also included in this monograph's findings.

Participation in Employer-Sponsored Training
In 1987, Nash and Hawthorne reported that firms themselves were by far the single most prevalent providers of corporate education to their employees. In 1975, 80 percent of all corporate dollars spent on human resource development went for in-house training; only 11 percent was spent on college tuition, and 9 percent went for outside courses (p. 8). This percentage has changed significantly since then. Why? The complexity of the environment an organization faces coupled with market competition and the firm's internal organization are now very significant determinants of training. These factors combined with practices such as total quality management (TQM) and work teams are predictive indicators of the amount of formal training provided (Cantor, 1997). In a corporate partnership for Continuous Quality Improvement (CQI/TQM) training between the Dallas County Community College District and Texas Instruments, for example, the college assists firms in providing the necessary quality assurance service to Texas Instruments's suppliers.

More firms report spending increased monies on education and training in recent years. Expenditures for corporate training in 1981 were $30 billion (Nash & Hawthorne, 1987), while training expenditures for U.S. business and industry in 1995 amounted to $55.3 billion (Bassi & Van Buren, 1998). These figures are supported by the Saratoga Institute's study (National Alliance of Business, 1997) and remained about the same for calendar year 1996. These figures represent an 84 percent increase in training expenditures by business and industry over 15 years. During calendar year 1997, on average almost 75 percent of a responding firm's employees received some form of adult education and training, a significant number for academic institutions that wish to include employees of local businesses and industries among the constituencies served by their institutions. Table 1 summarizes some of the major findings of the two ASTD studies with respect to training expenditures.

According to Bassi and Van Buren (1998, 1999), U.S. businesses spent 1.5 percent of their payroll on employee training in 1996 and 1.8 percent in 1997, for an average of $504 per employee in 1996 and $649 per employee the following year. "A recent survey by Arthur Andersen's Enterprise Consulting Group and National Small Business United reports that, on average, small and mid-sized companies are spending 2.7 percent of total revenue on employee training" (National Alliance of Business, 1997, p. 3). Further, "the Bureau of Labor Statistics survey indicates that the number of employees trained and the money spent on training grew in most organizations in the mid-1990s. In the three years preceding 1995, more than 69 percent of the companies reported increases in spending on formal training; 65 per-

TABLE 1

Corporate Training Expenditures

	1996	*1997*
Average total training expenditures (millions)	$1.4	$2.0
Average total training expenditures as percentage of payroll	1.5 percent	1.8 percent
Average total training expenditures per employee	$504	$649
Average percentage of employees trained	68.7 percent	74.3 percent
Sources: Bassi & Van Buren, 1998, 1999.		

cent reported increases in the percentage of employees trained over the same period" (Bassi & Van Buren, 1998, p. 27).

These expenditures underscore American businesses' increasing recognition of the value of investment in human resources and how training and education return dividends in terms of businesses' success. In fact, ASTD estimates that training expenditures grew by 18 percent from 1985 to 1997 after adjusting for inflation (National Alliance of Business, 1997).

Again, enlightened self-interest is a driving force. When businesses recognize that they can leverage monies spent on human resource development through partnerships with higher education, colleges and universities can not only increase their enrollments in programs but also become benefactors of grants of funds and equipment to embellish infrastructure. One such example is Microsoft's Working Connections information technology grants program (discussed later). Bassi & Van Buren (1998, 1999) also found that wages of training staff accounted for 39.2 percent of 1996 calendar year training expenditures and 41.4 percent of 1997 calendar year training expenditures. In addition, reimbursement of college tuition for employees accounted for 13.3 percent in calendar years 1996 and 1997, outsourcing of training another 26.2 percent in 1996 and 27.1 percent in 1997. These corporate training figures account for about 50 percent of America's total spending on higher education ("Learning Organizations," 1995). These data are significant for academic administrators to comprehend as they move toward developing partnerships and market their institutional capabilities for training to business. As seen herein, expenditures on higher education outside the academy have grown significantly. Bassi, Cheney, and Lewis (1998) suggest that the "chase" for qualified workers in our currently healthy economy is causing businesses to spend more liberally on human resource development.

In 1975, approximately 13 percent of employees working in firms with more than 500 employees participated in company-sponsored training (Nash & Hawthorne, 1987, p. 6). In contrast, more than 41 percent of American workers (approximately 46 million people) reported receiving corporate training from their company in 1991 (National Alliance of Business, 1997). The Bureau of Labor Statistics has found that larger firms (those employing 250 or more workers) are about one and a half times more likely to provide formal training for their employees than smaller firms. The BLS data also indicate that larger firms are twice as likely to provide training in job skills, 2.7 times as likely to provide workplace-related training, and 11 times as likely to provide training in basic skills than small firms (National Alliance of Business, 1997, p. 4). According to the Institute for Research on Higher Education (1997), "The fact is that *most* employers—over 75 percent in all—provide some type of tuition benefit to most types of workers, indicating a substantial demand for work-related education and training" (p. 40).

What does this trend indicate?

As companies face more intense competition, reorganize their workplaces and upgrade technology, they are investing more in education and training. After adjusting for inflation, training expenditures have grown by 18 percent during the last twelve years, according to ASTD estimates. NCEQW (National Center on the Educational Quality of the Workforce) found that 60 percent of the companies it surveyed are increasing training investments, while only 2 percent reported declines. (National Alliance of Business, 1997, p. 3)

NAB found that 69 percent of firms with fewer than 50 employees provided training, whereas 98 to 99 percent of firms with 50 to 250 employees provided training to their workers, suggesting that colleges or universities might better position themselves to serve smaller firms that do not have internal resources and capabilities to serve their employees. Colleges can help firms grow and develop their own best employees (Allen, 1996).

What kinds of firms provide training to their employees? Over the past several years, firms engaged in high-technology products and services spent by far the most on training and provided the greatest amount of education and training ($3.9 million in 1997). In 1997, employers in the TCPU sector outspent those in the FIRE sector, which had the second highest expenditures in 1996. Interestingly, the health care industry was rather low on the list in 1996 and continued to decrease its expenditures in this area in 1997. Nevertheless, as will be seen shortly, a very high percentage of health care workers do receive training.

> *Colleges or universities might better position themselves to serve smaller firms that do not have internal resources and capabilities to serve their employees.*

Industrial clusters are developed in a geographical area as a means to support a particular industry (Hoy, 1998). The Route 128–Boston information technology cluster is but one example. In addition to the computer hardware manufacturing industry located there, consulting firms, software firms, and educational institutions have located to support their customers and partners. There is a growing practice of colleges and universities helping business sectors organize for education and training by sponsoring and developing industry consortia, often collocated within a geographical cluster (Northeast Utilities System, 1998). In such an arrangement, an industry sector, such as the semiconductor industry, forms itself into a consortium for education and training. SEMATECH, the semiconductor education and training consortium, is discussed later.

For colleges wishing to extend their services to industry, knowing where to focus efforts is useful information. Table 2 presents data on training dollars and targeted learners in 1997.

Next, the data are analyzed according to the categories of workers per industry sector who receive education and

TABLE 2

Total Training Expenditures, by Industry Sector

	Total Training Expenditures ($ millions)	Total Training Expenditures Per Employee ($)	Percent of Employees Trained	Payments to Outside Vendors as Percentage of Expenditures
Information technology	3.9	943	70.3	35.3
TCPU	3.8	1,004	86.5	24.5
Government	2.6	514	70.7	26.8
Trade	2.5	412	69.5	16.1
FIRE	1.9	737	70.3	22.4
Agriculture/mining/ construction	0.6	686	79.9	40.6
Nondurable manufacturing	1.0	588	69.8	34.8
Durable manufacturing	1.2	488	72.9	35.5
Services	1.1	583	72.1	26.2
Health care	0.8	345	87.9	12.2

Source: Bassi & Van Buren, 1999.

training. U.S. Department of Labor statistics show that 60 percent of today's American workers are skilled, another 20 percent are professional, and the remaining 20 percent are unskilled (Evelyn, 1999). Typically, workers in more professional and technical categories have received training, but according to Table 3, this situation is changing. More production and hourly workers are now receiving training.

The percentage of employees trained, by industry sector, is shown in Table 4. These figures confirm the growing number of institutions that have embraced the movement toward development of education and training programs in support of certifying industry skill (see also "Academe's Response").

TABLE 3

Percentage of Workers Receiving Training

	Percentage	*Hours*
Managerial/administrative	87	4.3
Professional/technical	95	22.3
Sales/clerical	89	10.2
Service	71	5.6
Production/maintenance	80	15.2

Source: Adapted from National Alliance of Business, 1997, p. 5.

TABLE 4

Percentage of Employees Trained, by Industry Sector

Industry Sector	*1996*	*1997*
Health care	82	87.9
TCPU	72	86.5
High technology	71	70.3
Light manufacturing	68	69.8
FIRE	67	70.3
Business services	66	72.1
Heavy manufacturing	65	72.9
Construction	65	79.9
Customer service	62	—

Sources: Bassi & Van Buren, 1998, 1999.

Prominent Areas of Training and Education in Industry

Most of the corporate expenditures for education in the late 1970s went to functional technical training, amounting to 74 percent of the money spent and 61 percent of the students enrolled (Nash & Hawthorne, 1987). In addition, 24 percent of the expenditures went to and 37 percent of the students were enrolled in managerial training and education. Developmental education accounted for 2 percent of the students and expenditures during that time (p. 11).

Over the years, academia has been chastised for its often sluggish response to business and industry's need for worker training. To address such concerns, it is useful to understand industry's patterns of involvement in training as well as its particular needs and requirements. Tables 2 and 4 show that the largest percentage of trained employees was in the health care industry. Training in management/ supervisory skills and computer skills followed technical skills in both years. By type of course, technical skills were most frequently offered across all industry clusters in both years.

The ASTD survey uncovered some interesting trends and changes in curricula sponsored by business and industry over the past several years. Table 5 illustrates percentages of training dollars spent, by course type.

Claggett and Alexander (1995) indicate that 74 percent of the training provided by community colleges to business and

TABLE 5

Course Types as Percentage of Training Expenditures

Course	Percent
Job-specific technical skills	17
Management/supervision skills	12
Computer literacy	12
Orientation of new employees	12
Occupational safety and compliance	8
Professional skills	7
Customer skills	7
Sales	6
Quality	5
Source: Bassi & Van Buren, 1998.	

industry is aimed at upgrading employees' training, but a lesser emphasis, according to Table 5, has been on managerial training (perhaps because traditional universities now supply more management education), and at the time of the study, increased training was offered in technical and computer areas. This trend continued in 1997. "The distribution of expenditures mirrors fairly closely the distribution we observed last year where we examined the percentage of training time devoted to each subject area" (Bassi & Van Buren, 1999, p. 11). And Beckman and Doucette (1993) found in an earlier study that job-specific training was the type of training most often provided to business by the community colleges.

Based on these data, all other skills courses, including basic and enabling skills, quality, compliance, sales, and customer services, represented 6 percent or less of training dollars spent. Businesses can work with their local college or university to competitively acquire such training services.

External Providers of Training and Education

As we move toward a perspective on the growth and development of higher education outside the academy, an understanding of the trends affecting providers of training and education for business and industry is essential. Table 6 shows sources of staff training.

TABLE 6

Sources of Staff Training

Sources of Training	1996	1997
Employees at this location	95 percent	93 percent
Training companies	73 percent	77 percent
Independent consultants	68 percent	73 percent
Product suppliers	53 percent	60 percent
Employees at other locations	49 percent	NR
Other educational institutions	48 percent	54 percent
Community colleges	42 percent	49 percent
Union, trade, or professional organizations	17 percent	24 percent
Government organizations	12 percent	21 percent
Other	4 percent	NR

Note: NR = Not reported.

Sources: Bassi & Van Buren, 1998, 1999.

While the data suggest that in-house staff are still the primary source for staff training within a firm, outsourcing of training services is growing rapidly. The use of colleges, including community colleges, is on the rise for outsourcing training. Gose (1999) provides insights on the growth of continuing education services provided by colleges to business and industry. No longer viewed as an adjunct to the mission of the institution itself, continuing education and extended studies divisions of these institutions now represent a significant opportunity to generate operating capital for a college. Gose reports that New York University generates $92 million in yearly revenues through this division, and Harvard University takes in $150 million. Given this kind of potential, academic administrators need to understand the trends in outsourcing in business and industry and take the steps necessary to position their institution to benefit in kind.

Part of what needs to be understood is the way a potential partnering firm's training or human resource department is organized. ASTD research data indicate that 58 percent of large U.S. firms have downsized their training departments. Firms, large and small, are finding new ways to deliver quality instruction and creating structures to coordinate various vendors. The size and composition of corporate training departments are changing dramatically (Bassi & Van Buren, 1998).

Outsourcing of training services is growing rapidly.

Of significance to academics is that outsourcing training programs, including hiring consultants as trainers, is becoming more prevalent. While more use is being made of colleges for services delivered outside the academy, senior colleges are the least used providers of courses and training (National Alliance of Business, 1997, p. 6). Two-year institutions have become more aggressive in marketing their services. These figures have increased greatly from Nash and Hawthorne's study, where as high as 26 percent of employees were identified as attending formal collegiate courses as part of formal corporate training. Outsourcing is happening for many reasons, including accountability and costs. Where outside vendors are able to provide benchmarks of performance outcomes as part of their service agreements, training managers are using them to justify their services in the firm. Additional data provided by the National Alliance of Business with regard to outside training providers are shown in Table 7 to underscore the findings of a trend toward higher education outside the academy. The data in Table 7

TABLE 7

Use of Outside Training Providers

	Percent
Equipment vendors	50
Private consultants	36
Private industry councils/industry associations	34
Technical/vocational institutions	33
Community colleges	30
Senior colleges	20
Government funded	12
Unions	5

Source: Adapted from National Alliance of Business, 1997.

also support the notion of a trend toward outsourcing of technical skills training and increased use of higher education institutions for education and training services. Price et al. (1995) underscored the changing of ways and means by which community colleges approach business with their services.

According to Ouellette (1998):

The latest trend is to negotiate outsourcing contracts in which a university provides courses and technical degrees customized for a particular business. . . . According to a survey of 100 business trainers, 40% of large corporate training groups plan to create corporate/university partnerships this year [1998]. The survey found that by 2000, more than half of this custom training will be delivered via computer technologies such as the Internet and videoconferencing. (p. 20)

Predominant Methods of Instruction

Can academe learn from business and industry's experience with alternative methods for training delivery? Certainly, quickly emerging developments in computer technology and associated Internet/Web technology are revolutionizing training delivery. These technologies are catalyzing partnerships of traditional higher education, the private training vendor market, and business and industry. The 1998 ASTD survey (Bassi & Van Buren, 1998) found that the learning technologies shown in Table 8 were predominant.

TABLE 8

Use of Learning Technologies

	Percentage of Organizations Using
Presentation methods	
CBT (text only)	47.5
Multimedia	58.1
Interactive TV	14.3
Teleconferencing	31.4
Groupware	22.4
Virtual reality	2.7
Distribution methods	
Cable TV	6.4
CD-ROMs	49.2
E-mail	33.8
Internet	19.1
Simulators	20.6
World Wide Web	18.7

Source: Bassi & Van Buren, 1998.

In the most recent study, Bassi & Van Buren (1999) found no relationship between the extent of instructor-led, classroom-based training and outsourcing. But they observed that "organizations delivering a greater share of their training via learning technologies were more likely to use outside training providers" (p. 11). In addition, information technology was most often delivered in the classroom, although classroom training time as a percentage of training time has continued to decrease in the last several years (see Table 9). Learning technologies in business and industry might be emerging more quickly than in traditional academic institutions. Academic administrators must recognize this situation as one major reason for business to develop internal and alternative processes for educating and training employees.

At the time Nash and Hawthorne wrote their report (1987), corporate colleges numbered about 400. Today, there are several thousand corporate colleges in existence, in a number of different organizational configurations. Corporate colleges provide education and training services to their institutional sponsors. In addition to specific

TABLE 9

Training Time, by Delivery Method

Delivery Method	*Percent*
Traditional classroom	78.0
Learning technologies	9.0
Other self-paced methods	7.0
Other methods	6.0
Source: Bassi & Van Buren, 1999.	

education and training services and programs, some are affiliated with traditional institutions of higher education and can grant college credit and degrees to employees as students. Others, initially started as corporate training centers, have earned designations as higher education institutions and now grant degrees. Higher education outside the academy is a growing trend.

Summary

The data presented in this section offer evidence that the last half of the 1990s saw an unprecedented transformation of corporate training. At the beginning of the 20th century, American business and industry paid little attention to the development of corporate human resources. Toward the latter part of the century, the literature surrounding business growth and development suggests that human resources played an important part of businesses' success in a service economy—especially in an economy segueing into the information age.

The literature reviewed suggests several practices and trends:

- Business and industry have increased their spending on the workforce to ensure quality performance.
- Firms in high-technology industries are spending significant monies to maintain a skilled workforce.
- Corporate America increasingly is turning to sources outside business and industry to educate and train its workforce in order to obtain quality educational services at competitive prices.

- American businesses now recognize the need to be learning organizations in order to compete in a global economy.
- Higher education—more specifically community and technical colleges—is becoming the provider of choice to educate American workers.

The corporate university is quickly becoming the institutional configuration for educating and training workers. This institution is evolving in a number of ways, as discussed in the following section.

THE PRIVATIZATION OF HIGHER EDUCATION

In addition to the plethora of businesses that provide training for their employees, the 1990s witnessed growth in the number of private and proprietary and nonprofit institutions offering collegiate-level education to a growing number of nontraditional students. Hence, these institutions have identified significant niche markets as a result of college students' changing demographics and demands. The traditional university is no longer without competition for a student body: Witness the convergence of learning organizations, including museums, profit-making organizations, publishers, and others. This section reviews and analyzes the literature describing the expansion of privatization among higher education institutions.

The Driving Forces

Levine and Cureton (1998) advance the notion that a "living-learning" community characterized by the traditional university is disappearing on most campuses today. In its place is a "fast-food culture" in which students want an on-demand, no frills customer service approach to college services. These scholars cite statistics suggesting that fewer than one in six undergraduates today fits the stereotype of the 18- to 22-year-old American college student attending school full time and living on campus. "What this means is that higher education is not as central to the lives of today's undergraduates as it was to previous generations. Increasingly, college is just one of a multiplicity of activities in which they are engaged every day. For many, it is not even the most important of these activities; work and family often overshadow it" (p. 3).

Why does this professional working student gravitate to a proprietary institution of higher education rather than a traditional university charging less for its services? In part, students want from their colleges much the same things they want from their banks: an ATM on every corner, no lines to wait in, and 24-hour access to their money (Levine, 1998). And what they do not want their banks to offer is "softball leagues, religious counseling, or health services."

Students . . . want their colleges to be nearby and to operate at the hours most useful to them—preferably around the clock. They want convenience: easy, accessible parking (at the classroom door would not be bad);

no lines; and a polite, helpful, efficient staff. They also
want high-quality education but are eager for low
costs. For the most part, they are willing to comparison
shop, and they place a premium on time and money.
They do not want to pay for activities and
programs they do not use. (p. 4)

Today's students expect the same from their institutions
of higher education that they do from their retail shopping
establishments or health care institutions. They want value
for their time and money, and they do not want to pay for
services they do not want or cannot use. And they want it
with the speed the Internet offers.

Proprietary Schools Out in Front
Several colleges have emerged as major forces in the movement toward higher education outside the traditional academy. The University of Phoenix (UOP), part of the Apollo
Group, is the largest private university in the United States.
To meet the demands of the changing student population,
UOP has grown over the last two decades. The university
has 70 campuses and learning centers in 13 states. UOP's
average student is 35 years old, has an average family
income in excess of $60,000, and has about 13 years of
work experience (Klor deAlva, 1998).

According to Klor deAlva (1998), the University of
Phoenix meets these expectations for its 53,000 degree-
seeking students. Classes, typically held one evening a
week, are limited to an average of 13 students. Courses are
arranged in five- or six-week blocks or modules and
sequentially designed in the content area. Hence, students
can focus on one course of study at a time, building on that
knowledge base over the course of study. UOP's curricula
were developed in cooperation with the industries the
degree programs are intended to serve and are continually
updated to ensure relevance. "The courses are taught by
current industry leaders who offer the most effective
combination of academic theory and proven technique.
Therefore, what students learn in class today can be
immediately applied on the job tomorrow" (Klor deAlva,
1998, p. 16). A preponderance of today's students are career
oriented (Levine & Cureton, 1998) and see college as a
means to a career.

As of the time this monograph was written, several new ventures were organizing. One, the Open University of the United States (OUUS), is based on a sister institution in the United Kingdom and its concept of supported open learning. OUUS offers courses and degree programs, including a B.A. in English, humanities, international studies, liberal arts, social sciences, and business; a B.S. in computing and information technology; and an M.B.A. and M.S. in computing. OUUS is a not-for-profit corporation; it formed a partnership with Florida State University to offer a master's degree (see *www.fsu.edu/distance* and *www.open.ac.uk* for more information). Another, Harcourt, Inc., the publishing firm, has initiated Harcourt Learning Direct, a profit center under its Harcourt Higher Education Division. It is directed at delivering distance learning baccalaureate and graduate degree programs in business, health care administration, general studies, and information technology. The venture, as of the writing of this monograph, was working toward accreditation by the New England Association of Schools and Colleges (*Chronicle of Higher Education,* 1999, p. B35) (see *www.webct.harcourtcollege.com* for more information).

Sylvan Learning Systems, long recognized as a tutoring and testing proprietary organization, was also, as of the writing of this monograph, moving into the for-profit university market. According to Lively and Blumenstyk (1999), the firm is moving forward in a venture to create a chain of private colleges throughout Europe (p. A43). Its first site will be at the European University of Madrid, where it will acquire a controlling interest. The grand plan calls for embellishing the school's current programs and integrating some "American" programs in the professional disciplines through distance learning technologies with Caliber Learning Network. Caliber's partners include Johns Hopkins University and the University of Pennsylvania's Wharton School of Business. DeVry Inc. is an international educational system providing career-oriented bachelor's and master's degrees at more than 200 locations and has emerged as one of the largest proprietary degree-granting institutions in the United States and Canada. Listed on the New York Stock Exchange, it currently serves more than 38,000 students at 16 campuses. DeVry credits its success to being well positioned to meet students' needs and goals, specifically career-relevant undergraduate and graduate professional education leading to specific certifications, such as in information technology and electronics (R. Taylor, 1998). DeVry's academic baccalaureate career programs are offered year round, permitting a full-time student to complete the degree in three academic years (see *www.devry.com* for further information).

The Academy's Concerns and Its Response
Accreditation
What is likely to be the overall effect of the movement toward proprietary universities in any particular state? For a venture in higher education to be successful, it must be recognized by a regional accreditation association. A number of higher education ventures have been accredited, perhaps influenced by the pioneer, Western Governors University (Gehrke, 1998). The University of Phoenix has been regionally accredited by the Western Association of Schools and Colleges. As of the writing of this work, the commonwealth of Pennsylvania had approved an application for the University of Phoenix to offer programs in Pennsylvania (Selingo, 1999a). Likewise, the Open University of the United States has applied for accreditation from the Middle States Association of Schools and Colleges and at this point is working in a partnership arrangement with Florida State University and the California State University System. As more such ventures emerge and the various accreditation associations become more comfortable with private and historically nontraditional institutions moving into adult and higher education, regional accreditation of these programs is likely to become common (Selingo, 1999a). The question of development of broader and maybe national or international accreditation or accreditation standards remains to be answered.

Measures of quality
The University of Phoenix argues that quality is of the utmost importance in its higher education model. Similar to traditional institutions, its college faculty all hold doctoral or master's degrees in their respective disciplines. Unlike at traditional universities, however, all UOP faculty are adjunct and must be currently employed in the discipline in which they teach. All UOP faculty must complete a preemployment training program in instructional pedagogy (Klor deAlva, 1998). DeVry recruits and hires faculty, both full time and

part time, much like a traditional university. DeVry's faculty must hold appropriate academic and professional credentials (R. Taylor, 1998)

Accreditation of proprietary higher education is of concern to those studying this movement. The University of Phoenix is accredited by the Commission on Institutions of Higher Education of the North Central Association of Colleges and Schools. Its programs in nursing, which lead to Bachelor of Science in Nursing and Master of Science in Nursing degrees, are accredited by the National League for Nursing. The counseling program is accredited by the Council for Accreditation of Counseling and Related Educational Programs (see *www.uophx.com* for more information).

The plethora of colleges offering credit-bearing instruction over the Web has caused regional higher education accrediting organizations to give credence to the use of this technology in colleges and universities. In 1999, the first such accrediting organization to recognize on-line course delivery was the North Central Association of Colleges and Schools (Blumenstyk, 1999a).

Other proprietary institutions of higher education offer very specialized programs leading to advanced degrees. The Fielding Institute is one such institution. It describes itself as a "scholar-practitioner model designed to serve mid-career professionals who must maintain multiple commitments to family, work and community while earning an advanced degree" (see *http://www.fielding.edu/public/academic.htm* for more information). The Fielding Institute reflects all the requisite accreditation and professional recognition necessary to operate as a respectable institution of higher education. The Accrediting Commission for Senior Colleges and Universities of the Western Association of Schools and Colleges accredits the institute, the American Psychological Association accredits the graduate psychology program, and the school is a member of the National Council of Schools of Professional Psychology, among other such organizations (for more information, see *www.fielding.edu*).

The Internet and distance learning

Blumenstyk (1998) poses a question to the academic community: Is Microsoft your college's next competitor? With the proliferation of computer technologies, those organizations are reaching out to provide instruction over the Internet. More and more colleges are contracting with firms specializing in distance learning (mostly Internet-based) technologies. Firms such as Educational Video Conferencing are providing colleges and their faculties with customized training and multimedia development, electronic performance support systems, and Web-based test authoring and instructional delivery systems (see *http://www.evcinc.com* for more information). Learning Ventures also offers fully accredited on-line graduate degrees through its Graduate School of America. This proprietary institution of higher education has received accreditation through the North Central Association of Colleges and Schools (Blumenstyk, 1999a).

The information technology age has brought together the higher education community and the information technology industry. Partnerships such as Microsoft Corporation and approximately 17 community colleges in a Working Connections project demonstrate the power of public-private partnerships for design and development of curriculum and faculty training (for more information about the Working Connections program, see *www.microsoft.com* or *www.aacc.nche.edu*).

Yet significant issues are still to be fully addressed and resolved, including ownership of on-line courses. Drexel University, as of the writing of this monograph, was debating the issue (Blumenstyk, 1999b). Drexel's position, similar to other universities, is that ownership of faculty-developed on-line courses belongs to the university. No doubt such issues will ultimately require adjudication.

Ownership of curriculum

A primary concern of academe when partnering with business and community organizations for delivery of education and training external to the college is ownership of curriculum. Certainly if the college is to recognize formal courses of study as part of its offerings for degrees or certification, quality control is of paramount concern.

Johns Hopkins University joined a venture with Caliber Learning Network to offer a graduate medical education program from a distance (Magotte, 1999). The four-course certificate program is designed to meet the needs of physicians for medical management education. Caliber's approach is to use both synchronous and asynchronous

The information technology age has brought together the higher education community and the information technology industry.

media involving a combination of satellite transmission, compressed video teleconferencing, Web-based courses, e-mail, and the like. It draws international students. Described by Magotte as a win-win partnership, the university designed the academic content for the program, and the corporate partner focuses its attention on delivery. Caliber, Inc., is a public firm that grew out of a partnership between MCI and Sylvan. Other schools in partnership with Caliber include the University of Pennsylvania's Wharton School of Business and Teachers College, Columbia University (see *www.caliberlearning.com* for more information). Table 10 presents a cross section of other such ventures.

We are witnessing a plethora of Web-based course delivery ventures. One such venture, Connected Education, is an independent educational corporation chartered in New York State. In operation since 1985, it offers on-line courses for academic credit in cooperation with faculty from several traditional universities, including Polytechnic University of New York. University faculty develop the courses and place them on Connected Education's Website (*http://www.cinti.com/connect-ed/ welcome*). More than 2,000 students from more than 40 states have taken both undergraduate and graduate courses through the organization. Connected Education offers the traditional university community additional services, including tutoring in English as a second language, foreign language workshops, and on-line database searching.

OnLine Education, another virtual venture, was among the first commercial ventures to offer degree courses on line via computers. Marketing their products to working professionals, this firm developed the international professional student market as early as 1993. Initially, Oxford Brookes University in Great Britain partnered with OnLine Education to offer degrees to distance learning students (see *www.brookes.ac.uk* for more information). Other traditional university partners now include international institutions of higher education such as Charles Stuart University and the University of Lincolnshire & Humberside (see *http://www.online.edu* for more information). PRIMEDIA Corporate University Network also markets to working professionals (*http://www.exencom*), offering

TABLE 10

Higher Education–Proprietary Distance Learning Partnerships

College/ University	Proprietary Partner	Programs	Accreditation
American Coastline University	Incorporated as a nonprofit educational corporation	B.A., M.A. in cooperation with NY Regents, T. A. Edison, and others	CA Council on Private Postsecondary Education
Polytechnic University	Connected Education is an independent educational corporation	Courses at B.A., M.A. level	Middle States via university partner
Bath College of Higher Education			
New School for Social Research			
Anne Arundel Community College	PBS Corporation for Public Broadcasting	Complete A.A. program, B.A. courses/ programs	New England Association & Middle States via partners
Charter Oak State College			
Weber State University	National Universities Degree Consortium	B.A., M.A., Ed.S.	All via partner colleges
University of Maryland			
Kansas State University			
Washington State University and others			
George Washington University	Jones Education Company	B.A. Business Communications, certificate programs	All via partner colleges
University of Colorado			
California State at Dominguez Hills			
Pennsylvania State University	AT&T Learning Network	CEU and undergraduate courses	Middle States

Web-based and satellite instructional technologies (see *www.Primediaventures.com* for more details).

Online Learning.net is another proprietary Internet course delivery management and marketing enterprise that partnered with UCLA Extension (a self-supporting division of UCLA) several years ago. Profitability and quality program delivery are essential components of this institution. UCLA wanted a partner that could provide a workable software platform, marketing and promotional assistance, and technical support for students, customers, faculty, and staff. About 100 courses a quarter for teachers, in-service teachers, and teachers of English as a second language are offered to students and customers in 50 states and 40 countries.

Jones Education Company, a proprietary firm in partnership with George Washington University and others, offers externally delivered college courses leading to undergraduate and graduate degrees using videotapes and the Internet. In this arrangement, the private sector offers its technology-based consulting services to traditional higher education institutions to develop or convert courses to a medium useful for distance learning, such as Web-based technology. The firm and the college comarket the courses, which become part of the college's offerings and are taught by the college's faculty, making them creditable to the college's accredited degrees. The firm receives a fee for each student served and each course sold (see *www.jec.edu* for more details).

The AT&T Learning Network Virtual Academy, a relatively new venture offering a series of on-line courses ranging from continuing professional education to college courses, uses e-mail and video teleconferencing support (see *http://www.attcom/ learningnetwork* for more details).

As the movement toward use of technology to facilitate learning progresses, most traditional institutions of higher education are analyzing their institutional and student needs to determine the best way to enter the milieu of technological literacy. In some cases, partnerships of proprietary firms and colleges provide a means to solve the problem. In other instances, consortia of traditional colleges and universities join ventures to offer services while reaching new nontraditional students.

As shown in Table 10, numerous traditional colleges have chosen to partner with distance learning firms and/or other colleges to extend their courses to a growing non-traditional student market. A participating college is able to gain the consulting services of professional instructional designers and instructional technologists to convert a course to a Web-based medium via the consortium and then market the course to a wider student constituency via the consortium. Each college reaches a larger potential audience and shares in the costs of Web-based course development.

College and university administrators are attempting to be proactive in responding to students' demands for access to Web-based distance learning. The National Universities Degree Consortium (NUDC), a consortium of 12 traditional universities, was developed to maximize faculty efforts at course development via the Internet. NUDC offers nontraditional students opportunities to pursue college courses at a distance using the Internet (see *http://www.sc.edu/deis/NUDC* for more information). NUDC publishes a catalog and student handbook describing the process required to take courses through participating colleges and to earn a degree at a distance from Charter Oak State College, Empire State College, or Thomas Edison State College (see *www.sc.edu/deis/nudc* for more details).

Relevant technical education

Part of the dilemma faced by colleges and universities that offer programs in technology and preparation of the workforce is keeping current with the requirements of the particular discipline respective to curricula. As discussed, the University of Phoenix addresses these issues through exclusive use of practicing professionals as both curriculum designers and teaching faculty.

Similar to DeVry Inc., ITT Technical Institutes has emerged as a leader in postsecondary education focused specifically on technology-oriented programs of study. The programs at ITT lead to associate, bachelor's, and master's degrees.

Many colleges have formed partnerships with proprietary technical schools to offer up-to-date and relevant technical programs. Dabney S. Lancaster Community College and Blue Ridge Community College (both in Virginia) partner with a proprietary tractor trailer driving school to offer training in driving 18-wheelers to local community college students. Neither college could provide such training independently because of the costs of such a program and lack of instructors. Likewise, Naugatuck Valley Community College in Connecticut partners with New Horizons Computer Learning Center to offer Microsoft Certified Systems Engineer computer training. Again, without the instructors recruited and employed by New Horizons, the college alone could not offer technically relevant instruction.

Ancillary and support services

Traditional university ancillary and support services have been privatized for some time. More recently, the developmental studies programs of some colleges and universities have moved outside academe. One firm that has moved rapidly into this venue is Kaplan Educational Services, Inc. According to Rosen (1998), this for-profit firm has established a niche in the higher education market by providing assistance in remediation of students' deficiencies in basic academic skills, thus aiding in the retention of students at traditional colleges and universities. Such a partnership can be viewed, according to Rosen, as a model for the private firm helping the academic institution. Greenville Technical College and Chattanooga State Technical Community College, for instance, have contracted with Kaplan Educational Services for remedial education services. At Greenville, developmental education faculty have worked with Kaplan's staff to develop effective instructional strategies for learners, including retention strategies and seminars on teaching techniques for in-service faculty. At Chattanooga, the Kaplan partnership has resulted in development of more refined student assessment instruments and a program for development of customized instructional materials.

Certainly Microsoft is large enough to create a Microsoft University if such a venture were its goal. The firm reportedly has been looking at course content and instructional techniques for acquisition and has spoken with selected institutions about instructional techniques and processes, such as for teaching foreign languages, that can be useful in developing instructional software, perhaps as a joint venture (Blumenstyk, 1998). The products already on the market in the learning arena are quite popular and user friendly

Certainly most of the impetus for partnerships with external business and community constituents is the need of traditional academic institutions to raise operating funds separate from those derived from conventional sources.

(e.g., Encarta Virtual Globe). Software firms can indeed be competitors to traditional higher education.

Microsoft, however, is reportedly seeking out partnerships to coexist with higher education in a collaborative rather than competitive environment. Through its Microsoft Partners program, the corporation seeks to address the shortage of workers in information technology through grants to higher education institutions to develop information technology programs and recruit minority and special population students. Jones Education Company provides insights into Microsoft Partners's goals and objectives and its overall motivation for partnering with higher education. First, Microsoft understands that a partnership leverages the power of its own staff and that of its partners in providing training for young learners, thus reaching diverse student populations, geographies, and age groups. Second, Microsoft understands that community colleges in particular are well positioned to reach these populations and that two-year institutions are significant providers of instruction in information technology. And third, Microsoft believes that it can best respond to local business needs through such higher education partnerships.

Profits and enrollments

Not to be forgotten are the fiscal aspects of operating a college today. Certainly most of the impetus for partnerships with external business and community constituents is the need of traditional academic institutions to raise operating funds separate from those derived from conventional sources. As Blumenstyk (1999b) notes, however, the marketing of distance learning does not sit well with all faculty. Issues such as cost and control of course content are at the forefront of college senate debates nationwide. Add such issues as faculty load, development time, and budgets, and one can quickly see that change and distance learning will not come easily to all institutions.

In each case cited herein, arrangements call for the college to share in the fees and charges for services. For the truck driving school, for example, students' payments are made directly to the commercial school, with the commercial school paying per capita fees to the college plus rentals for the college classroom. In the case of the New Horizons partnership, the college charges students an aggregate tuition, part of which is remitted to the commercial vendor based on enrollments. In every case, the college realizes needed operating revenues while providing vitally needed services to its community.

Summary

This section has highlighted the growth of proprietary ventures in higher education and the impetus for such growth and development. It has reviewed and discussed for-profit institutions of higher education that have evolved to provide no frills courses and programs aimed at degrees. The section has also highlighted the proprietary ventures that have developed to offer traditional colleges ancillary services in distance learning via the Web and in developmental studies. Significantly, it has also presented the controversy and concerns expressed by traditional academic establishments about proprietary ventures and their ultimate effects on traditional higher education.

ACADEME'S RESPONSE: Building Partnerships With Industry

The search for alternative sources of funding to operate the academy has caused both administrators and faculty to re-think their relationships with their corporate neighbors (Aronowitz, 1998). This section looks at how colleges and businesses have come together to solve mutual problems of educating a citizenry and a workforce. It looks at programmatic partnerships in areas with high demand for workers. Programs such as the Microsoft partnership, Cisco Systems' Academic Partners, and others are quickly proliferating among information technology vendors (Cantor, 1998, 1999). This section also looks at processes and conventions that have evolved in the academy in order to recognize industry or corporate training as part of the academic degree program. Many of these conventions were first discussed in Nash and Hawthorne's work (1987), and they have survived and been further developed in the two plus decades since.

This section presents two predominant forms of response on the part of higher education to the challenges presented by external programs of study. One form has been through partnerships with business and industry to provide contract training to meet specific needs of the workplace. The second has been by developing mechanisms to recognize education and training provided by organizations external to the traditional academy. Let's first look at partnerships.

Industry comes together with higher education when there exists a quid pro quo (Braun & Arden, 1998; Bishop, 1996). In the case of the semiconductor manufacturing industry over the last several years, a shortage of technicians has threatened the industry's ability to meet market demands. As a result, a group of the major semiconductor manufacturers joined together to establish an educational corporation named SEMATECH. Through SEMATECH, the ten largest semiconductor manufacturers, including Intel and Motorola, were able to partner with community colleges such as Maricopa Community College in Arizona to develop state-of-the-art programs of study to prepare the kind of specialized technicians manufacturers need (Cantor, 1998). SEMATECH is a model for collaborations of industry and higher education for high-tech education and training of the workforce. SEMATECH also received a grant from the National Science Foundation to underwrite faculty and course development through Maricopa Community College. As of the writing of this monograph, SEMATECH had joined with colleges nation-wide in geographical areas where manufacturing plants exist to offer educational programs. Colleges in Massachusetts, Virginia, California, New Mexico, Texas, and Arizona have become involved with the program. SEMATECH representatives from industry and higher education review an applicant college's programs and plans to incorporate the SEMATECH courses of study, and faculty credentials and willingness to be further trained in the technology before ultimately endorsing the college as a SEMATECH education and training provider. Local industry cooperates with colleges in providing the technician-level course of study, which includes A.S. and B.S. programs in semiconductor manufacturing and electronics and semiconductor engineering. Local cooperation includes providing student and faculty internships and advice on the curriculum (see *http://www.so.cc.va.us* and *www.peabody.gc.maricopa.edu/tech/smt.htm* for more information).

Growth of Information Technology

Other industries have also seen the need to partner with colleges to ensure that graduates of their programs are prepared for the rigors of the workplace. In the information technology arena, Cisco Systems Corp., the manufacturer of computer networking technologies, developed its Cisco Networking Academy program. The program brings together Cisco and its resellers, high schools, and two- and four-year colleges to offer an industry-developed course of study leading to college degrees and industry certifications. At the center of the Networking Academy program is the Area Networking Academy, which is generally a senior-level higher education institution, such as Alfred University in New York. The Area Networking Academy faculty train and mentor Regional Networking Academy faculty, who are generally faculty from a community college, such as Norwalk Community College in Connecticut. Regional Networking Academy faculty, in turn, train and mentor Local Networking Academy faculty, who are generally at high schools—for example, in Stamford, Connecticut (Cantor, 1999; Santamaria, 1998).

Cisco developed a program consisting of a planned series of courses in networking technology that begins in high school and bridges into a community college associate degree in computer systems. This program model includes a structured internship in a cooperating industry. The model provides for a bridge beyond the associate degree into a baccalaureate degree with participating senior higher education institutions. The Cisco Networking Academy program curriculum supports competency certifications for Cisco's workers. The first level of certification, the Cisco Certified Networking Associate (CCNA), parallels the series of courses from high school to community college. The next level, the Cisco Certified Networking Professional (CCNP), parallels the transition from community college to baccalaureate program. The third level, the Cisco Certified Internetworking Engineer (CCIE), parallels the transition from baccalaureate to graduate education. The Cisco Certified Networking Associate certification is offered to students who complete the program of study through Sylvan Learning Centers (Cantor, 1999; Nimtz, Coscarelli, & Blair, 1995).

Cisco provides the community college with laboratory equipment and training for the community college faculty. The community college faculty, in turn, recruits local high school partners and trains and mentors the high school faculty. Changes in technology and subsequent course content are then provided to the community college faculty to relay to the high school faculty. Cisco Networking Academy programs have been adopted statewide in several states, including Virginia and Wisconsin.

In a similar effort, Microsoft recently launched its Microsoft networking specialist program, which is an effort to partner with higher education (Rosa, 1998). Offered through Microsoft's authorized academic training program and Microsoft Press, this program is intended to help community colleges and secondary schools and offer networking education and training to their students and meet the demand for more than a half million workers over the next several years (see *www.microsoft.com/education* for more details).

Oracle Corporation, Novell Corporation, and Microsoft each have a program open to higher education institutions. Although each program differs in structure, each is aimed at linking industry to academic institutions and helping academe extend into the community with technology-oriented education and training for the local workforce (Patterson, 1996; Yates, 1999). Oracle, through its education outreach division, Oracle University, offers a workforce development program for community college partners. Through this initiative, Oracle supports delivery of information technology programs through the community colleges. Oracle products are made available at substantial discounts to community college faculty, as is faculty training in these products through Oracle vendors. The products include Database Analyst/Business Analyst, Internet Java Developer, and Oracle Database Operator, paralleling the Oracle certifications (see *www. oracle.com* for further details about Oracle and *www.novell.com* for further information about the Novell program).

Advanced technology centers are another way in which colleges and universities can reach out into the greater community to offer relevant technology training in partnership with business and industry (Hunt, 1995). Advanced technology centers have become (1) catalysts for developing training programs for a highly skilled workplace, (2) a focal point for colleges' extension programs in industrial and engineering technology, (3) transition media from associate to bachelor's programs for students, (4) support for small businesses in training and consulting, (5) providers of TQM/CQI and related specialized training for businesses, and (6) nurturers of manufacturing partnerships and consortia. In 1988, nine sponsoring institutions formed the National Coalition of Advanced Technology Centers (1992), including Pikes Peak Community College (Colorado), Valencia Community College (Florida), Macomb Community College (Illinois), and Massachusetts Bay Community College (Massachusetts). Programs offered ranged from flexible computer-integrated manufacturing centers to manufacturing partnerships to apprenticeship programs in cooperation with degree programs. In all cases, local industry becomes a central focus and an integral part of the program (Doucette, 1997; Heide, 1997).

Growth of College Continuing Education and Extended Studies

Not all partnerships emanate from large national industries. Itawamba Community College in Mississippi has developed an extended education and training partnership with local Tecumseh Products Company. The college provides preemployment services to employees of the firm, basic education classes, technical training, apprenticeship programs, upgrading and retraining programs, and leadership and management training. The firm in turn has provided donations that have resulted in the college's developing its Advanced Manufacturing Center (Itawamba Community College, 1995). In fact, many similar efforts have been undertaken by colleges and universities through their extended studies and workforce education or continuing education divisions (Meighan, 1995).

The traditional academic community has become acutely aware of the competition to address the demands of an emerging student body that is aging and more preoccupied with life's demands (Levine, 1988). Higher education is no longer the principal focal point of this generation's college students. More and more, this student body wants an educational provider to offer its services in a streamlined fashion without frills or inconveniences. To these ends, alternative systems of higher education delivery have emerged.

Validating Higher Education Outside Academe
A significant amount of higher education outside traditional academe happens as a result of life's pursuits, including experience gained in the workplace. Higher education has not only come to recognize this but also, in recent years, actually embraced this reality through organizations such as the American Council on Education (ACE). ACE's Center for Adult Learning and Educational Credentials sponsors the College Credit Recommendation Service, the Credit by Examination Program, and the Military Evaluations Program.

One means by which traditional universities can work with business and industry is through ACE's College Credit Recommendation Service (CCRS) (formerly Program on Noncollegiate Sponsored Instruction). Since 1974, this ACE program has enabled thousands of employees worldwide to receive the benefits of college credit for formal workplace education (see *http://www.ACENET.edu/programs/CALEC/ home.html* for further information). Military, corporate, and professional education and training can be reviewed by ACE-CCRS. Firms such as AT&T, the American Bankers Association, DANA Corporation, and Xerox Corporation have participated in the program. CCRS reviewers, people from both industry and education who are chosen and trained in the review process by ACE, recommend whether

Higher education is no longer the principal focal point of this generation's college students.

or not to grant college credits for a course and, if so, how many. "Through this program, faculty members from a college or university evaluate the training courses offered by an organization and make college credit recommendations when appropriate. Individuals who complete the training course can then take the recommendation to a college or university and ask if the school will recognize the course for credit" (Kurschner, 1997, p. 52).

CCRS has bridged academia and the workplace by providing a mechanism for validating the quality of education and training in the workplace. It has created a means by which employees can receive college credits for formal employer-sponsored training. By doing so, employees can segue into formal collegiate programs and reduce the employer's cost of reimbursement for college courses. For the college, it provides a valuable link to business and industry.

ACE publishes its *National Guide to Educational Credit for Training Programs* annually. This guide lists the industry-sponsored training programs for which CCRS recommendations have been made, along with the criteria (applicable courses and degree levels) for each recommendation. Courses are reviewed periodically, and recommendations change.

Illinois-based Productivity Point International has used this program to facilitate its employees' earning college credit for in-house training. Similarly, Pacific Bell "has joined a growing list of more than 250 U.S. organizations that have received 'college credit recommendations' on training courses they offer to employees, clients, and association and union members" (Kurschner, 1997, p. 52).

The CCRS program has helped businesses save significant amounts of money on the reimbursement of college tuition for employees as well as provided the portability of college credentials to employees who might need to change jobs because of fluctuating economic conditions (Kurschner, 1997). Interestingly, the California State University System has developed a competing college credit recommendation process for business and industry, which has cultivated the favor of approximately 1,400 colleges and universities nationwide.

Military Education and the Traditional College
Academe has long recognized military education and training. "A recently concluded study comparing the education

levels of army brigadier generals with those of corporate managers and executives revealed that substantially more officers held master's degrees. The number of officers holding Ph.D. degrees was only slightly [fewer] than the number of private sector executives and managers with doctorates" (Eurich, 1990, p. 152). The U.S. military has long recognized the value of continuing professional education and to that end has supported higher education partnerships with traditional institutions as well as run its own institutions of higher education (such as the U.S. Naval Academy and the U.S. Military Academy).

Partnerships of formal military education and training and higher education have recently taken the form of a Naval Recruiting Command project to formally link selected community college technology degree programs with the Navy's basic and specialized technician training. Students in community colleges can be afforded naval career opportunities with associated educational benefits. For example, a student enters the community college on a Navy educational deferment and pursues two semesters of college courses. Upon completion of the yearlong college study, the student enters the Navy and completes the technical training. Upon completion of the Navy training, the student gains the appropriate rank and earns an associate degree from the "home" college (Golfin & Curtin, 1998).

ACE also performs military training course and program evaluations similar to its corporate course recommendations. Since 1942, ACE has maintained a separate credit recommendation guide and an Army/ACE Registry Transcript System for military personnel. Transcripts are recognized by colleges and universities, and appropriate college credits can be posted to a student's transcript once the college has ascertained the appropriateness of military and/or corporate education and training toward a college degree.

Public Access and Television
Higher education outside the academy has also been promoted by entities such as public television. The Corporation for Public Broadcasting sponsors Public Broadcasting Service Online, an on-line medium that allows adults to pursue continuing higher education for credit through continuing education units or not for credit. Through its Going the Distance

project, a national effort by public television to assist colleges in developing distance degree programs, PBS has made higher education available to the nation's adult population at a distance. Going the Distance is a virtual campus with participating colleges throughout the United States. For example, Anne Arundel Community College in Maryland offers coursework toward associate degrees and certificates (in some cases complete programs) via Web courses, interactive courses, telecourses, and Weekend College (see *http://www.pbs.org/adultlearning/als/* for more information).

Health Care Institutions and Extended Studies

Continuing medical education (CME) is another variation of extended learning, often offered in cooperation with hospitals and health care organizations. The University of Rochester Medical Center, for example, offers continuing professional education in cooperation with the University of Rochester. Courses are accredited by the Accreditation Council for Continuing Medical Education. Physicians and other medical professionals rely on these courses to maintain their licensure and professional competency (see *http://www.urmc.rochester.edu/smd/CPE* for further information).

Adult Education Outreach

Traditional collegiate institutions recognized the need to serve a growing nontraditional student cohort as early as 1971 with the founding of Regents College, part of the State University of New York System. Regents College was "founded on the belief that what someone knows is more important than where and how the knowledge was acquired" (see *http://www.Regents.edu* for further information). Students enroll in courses that have been prepared in various self-study media. They are provided with a faculty mentor to monitor and assist them, and they exchange messages via telephone, fax, or e-mail.

Faculty are drawn from numerous other traditional colleges and universities. Regents College offers associate and baccalaureate degrees in business, liberal arts, nursing, and technology; it is accredited by the Commission on Higher Education of the Middle States Association of Colleges and Schools. Regents College has also embarked on a competency examination project in selected disciplines.

Colleges can use these validated examinations to assess a student's externally acquired knowledge and skills for college credit. The University of Maryland University College, Thomas A. Edison College in New Jersey, and Charter Oak College in Connecticut are other colleges that subscribe to this instructional model.

Continuing Education Units

College and university accrediting organizations such as the Southern Association of Colleges and Schools (SACS) have formally recognized the value of noncredit continuing education to lifelong education and career development. In that regard, continuing education units (CEUs) have emerged as a medium for recognizing and documenting the successful completion of noncredit courses of study. As early as 1971, SACS's Commission on Colleges adopted the following criteria for accreditation: "For noncredit continuing education programs, the institution should follow national guidelines for the awarding of Continuing Education Units" (Commission on Colleges of SACS, 1988, p. 7). The criteria outlined in SACS's policy provide for formal courses of study to be based on learning objectives; faculty credentials; instructional processes, content, and methodology; and student and program evaluation criteria. CEUs are recognized by professional organizations, licensing and certifying bodies, and employers concerned about employees' competence.

Role and Reactions of the Accrediting Agencies

Accreditation is important in working to integrate corporate-sponsored education and training into academic degree programs. It is a necessary aspect of the administration of extended studies programs. Collegiate accreditation organizations in the United States have had to pay attention to both the growth of corporate education programs and distance learning initiatives motivated by the advancement of the Internet and computer-based technologies.

Formal private higher education ventures such as DeVry, the University of Phoenix, and ITT Technical Institutes recognize the need to structure their operations so as to meet accreditation standards. For instance, ITT Technical Institutes has received accreditation for many of its schools from the Accrediting Commission of Career Schools and Colleges of Technology (see *http://www.ittech.edu* for further information). Other ITT schools are accredited by the Accrediting Council of Independent Schools and Colleges. The appropriate accrediting body for a school to work with often depends on the state where the school operates and the programs it offers.

For instance, the Commission on Technical and Career Institutions of the New England Association of Schools and Colleges considers applications from technical or career-level institutions of higher education, baccalaureate-granting institutions, and secondary applied technology centers and technical schools in the New England states. The commission sets forth criteria for the institution to review to determine its eligibility for consideration for accreditation (see *http://www.neasc.org/ctci/ctcielig.htm* for additional information). Accreditation must be renewed periodically under all accreditation program guidelines.

The accrediting bodies have begun to address standards that need to be developed and implemented to ensure quality in distance learning and Internet-delivered academic programming. This aspect of higher education administration and policy formulation is just beginning to take shape.

Summary

This section has examined the various initiatives undertaken by colleges and universities to build bridges with business and industry, military, and other organizations engaging in higher education for their constituencies. It has discussed the role of the various regional higher education accrediting agencies and their reactions to those initiatives.

THE CORPORATE RESPONSE: Partnerships of Business and Higher Education

This section reviews the literature describing the evolution and growth of the corporate university, an institution developed by corporations to meet business changes created by a global economy and increased competition. Nash and Hawthorne's original work (1987) identified about 400 firms that had initiated and developed corporate universities to educate and train their workforces. The impetus for the corporate university was to obtain quality educational services at competitive prices to maintain a skilled workforce and to create a learning organization that could compete in a global economy (Meister, 1998b; Bachler, 1997a). Through an understanding of the corporate university movement, the academic administrator can envision activities wherein the college's or university's mission can permit shared roles and activities with a corporate college.

> *A corporate university is the centralized strategic umbrella for the education and development of employees and value chain members such as customers, suppliers, and dealers. . . . Most importantly, a corporate university is the chief vehicle for disseminating an organization's culture and fostering the development of not only job skills, but also such core workplace skills as learning-to-learn, leadership, creative thinking, and problem solving.* (Meister, 1998a, p. 38)

As can be seen from this definition, many of its central elements correlate with the goals of the traditional university. Further, an understanding of the corporate university is important for the academic to comprehend so as to be in a position to plan and deliver programs to meet corporate needs (Gjertsen, 1997).

Corporate universities differ from traditional training departments in that traditional training departments tend to be reactive, decentralized, and aimed at a wide employee audience (Chase, 1998). Corporate universities are strategic institutions that shape corporate culture and foster the development of leadership, critical thinking, and problem solving (Sunoo, 1998).

Table 11 presents a breakdown of selected corporate universities by industry sector (Meister, 1998b). The table reflects a very small cross section of the more than 1,200 firms and organizations sponsoring corporate

TABLE 11

Selected Corporate Universities, by Industry Sector

Sector	Firm
High technology	AT&T School of Business and Technology
	Dell University
	Oracle University
FIRE	Bank of Montreal Institute for Learning
	Charles Schwab University
	MasterCard University
Business services	Arthur Andersen Center for Professional Development
	First University (First Union)
	Service Delivery University (Fidelity Investments)
Manufacturing	Raychem University
	Whirlpool Brandywine Performance Centre
	Saturn Training Center
TCPU	Sprint University of Excellence
	Verifone University
	TVA University
Health care	United HealthCare Learning Institute
	UCH Academy (Univ. of Chicago Hospital)
Customer service	MBNA Customer College

universities, but it illustrates the diversity of industries participating in such ventures.

Successful corporate universities are built on a number of basic foundational blocks:

- Program elements should align with the firm's business strategies. The education programs should provide skills and knowledge that will help the firm achieve its goals. Employees should realize that learning is connected to the firm's desired outcomes.
- The corporate university should provide varied learning opportunities and learning methodologies (including short courses, seminars, computer-based or Internet-based offerings, and on-the-job learning opportunities) (Gjertsen, 1997; Moore, 1997). Learned information and

skills must be immediately applicable to the employee's job and work responsibilities.

- Employees should have personal learning plans that help them understand the critical competencies necessary for job performance. Employees should be encouraged to manage their own personal professional development.
- Top corporate management must support the corporate university (Allen, 1996).

The corporate university should "act like 'corporate glue' by bringing people together from all of the company locations for a common learning experience" (Allen, 1996).

Profit-Making Opportunities
Corporate Universities International (1998a) produced a survey that provides an enlightening view of the state of the industry in corporate universities:

An increasing number of corporate universities are moving to accredit their customized curricula for college credit.

The late 1990s can be viewed as a turning point for corporate universities, as they have grown dramatically in number—topping 1,200—and have ascended in stature, within their respective organizations. Increasingly, corporate universities are being used as tools for change management. What's more, a growing number of corporate universities have begun developing alliances with institutions of higher education as the scope and type of corporate/college partnerships have expanded.

What is more, firms such as Disney, Motorola, and Saturn have initiated profit centers in their corporate university structures, licensing and selling education and training products to other firms and organizations. For example, "through a partnership with the Erie County Technical Institute and the Pennsylvania Department of Education, the Lord Institute has expanded its training programs to certification and degree programs targeting suppliers and distributors" (p. 1).

Moving closer to the benefits of traditional universities, an increasing number of corporate universities are moving to accredit their customized curricula for college credit. Approximately 25 percent of the more than 1,000 corporate universities also aspire to grant accredited degrees by 2005

(National Alliance of Business, 1997). The motivation for this benefit for employees is the desire to provide workers with portable credentials and give them added security in turbulent economic times.

Meister (1998a) notes that 40 percent of corporate universities queried in one survey indicated that they plan to grant degrees in partnership with accredited institutions of higher education. The drive behind this movement appears to be a growing interest in portable credentials afforded through accredited learning programs. Unlike a tuition reimbursement program, a corporate university is up front in specifying learning outcomes and skills needed by employees in the partnership arrangement between firm and college. Corporate partnerships with traditional universities succeed when both parties specify what they want from each other and plan for bridging the cultural differences that exist (p. 3).

Successful Management Practices and Future Directions for Corporate Universities

The 1998 survey of corporate universities (Meister, 1998a) found key successful management practices and future directions for corporate universities:

- Effectively manage the budget.
- Accelerate and experiment with technology for learning.
- Increase alliances with higher education institutions.
- Increase range of measurements for evaluating the effectiveness of the corporate university.
- Expand the scope of operations across the globe (pp. 3–4)

The survey findings align significantly with and complement the foundational blocks for a successful corporate university cited earlier. These foundational blocks can provide insights into how higher education is functioning outside the academy. The remainder of this section focuses on corporate university practices.

Effectively manage the budget

More than 30 percent of an annual training expenditure of $30 billion spent by U.S. businesses is spent on college education for workers, although this level of spending is expected to decrease as firms turn to in-house training to better meet their employees' training needs (Watson, 1995,

p. 50). The National Semiconductor University, for example, budgeted $1.5 million annually for on-site college degree programs (associate, bachelor's, and master's degrees), three times the amount it had previously spent on tuition reimbursement (Watson, 1995). Motorola University, according to Allen (1996), spends about $140 million a year on training, and for every $1 spent in training, $33 is returned to the company. At Motorola, all 132,000 employees, from chair to janitor, must take a minimum of 40 hours of job-related training annually. Sprint created its University of Excellence in 1990, primarily to serve as an internal company consultant to meet business goals of maximizing market share while reducing unit training costs (Mailliard, 1997).

Align program elements with the firm's business strategy

Motorola University's investment in training and education is driven by the philosophy that, to survive, product quality is a must and that, moreover, product quality comes from educated and trained workforces (Allen, 1996). This philosophy is echoed by Ford's Fairlane Training and Development Center. Fairlane fancies itself a school for "retooling" and "retrofitting" its employees (Allen, 1996). "We believe that we can get a sustainable competitive advantage if we develop and nurture those skills ourselves with a career-long approach" (p. 25).

The corporate university has become a medium for employees to "bond" with a firm or organization (Watson, 1995, p. 49). Southern Company College began its corporate university in 1991 with a mission specifically to "create an awareness of what would be required for the company to be successful in a changing environment," promoting the motto, "we champion and accelerate learning" (Allen, 1996, p. 61). A company official says, "The primary reason is to instill the knowledge and skills to add value to the company. We want to be competitive. We believe that the strongest change agent we have is to develop the culture we need in the coming environment" (p. 61). The corporate university was envisioned as a catalyst for facilitating such a business strategy through behavior changes on the part of the employees—which was best done by the firm's controlling education and training *internally*. As the company indicates, however, 67 percent of the training is delivered off site, much of it interactively using computers and satellite delivery and in many instances through distance technologies by college professors and others. In this way, a corporate university becomes an institution that crosses international boundaries, thus allowing firms with global markets to provide education and training to their employees and customers anywhere in the world.

Provide varied learning opportunities and methodologies

Citing results from her survey of corporate university activities, Sullivan (1998) discusses a transition from instructor-led training to self-paced learning and an increased presence of multiple media to accommodate diverse learning styles. Many corporate universities operating today offer training and education in varied modes and media. Most have formed alliances with other corporate universities in their industry through consortia or with traditional colleges for services and programs.

In some instances, business leaders view corporate-university partnerships as an opportunity to embrace new cultures and business methods and to bring desired change to the firm. The Daimler-Benz Corp. partnership with the University of Southern California is but one example.

> *The USC/Daimler-Benz partnership, like any such international alliance, has created a situation where two organizations representing different cultures may find themselves at odds with regard to their respective learning styles. . . . In Germany, you sit and listen, but here, our faculty expects students to participate. At first, not all of the students were happy about that, and it took them a while to get accustomed to it, but they ultimately adapted very well because in the German educational system, being prepared is paramount for success.* (Braun & Arden, 1998, p. 10)

Ensure top corporate managers support the corporate university

Sprint's University of Excellence was created in 1990 to develop a corporate culture aimed at melding diverse cultures among business units into one cohesive focus on customers (Mailliard, 1997). The university supports delivery of the corporate philosophy to Sprint's 47,000 employees. "The UE serves as an internal company consultant. We design the programs to meet our business goal of maximizing market share while appropriately reducing unit costs. Building core competencies helps us prepare employees to adapt and succeed in a competitive environment" (p. S6).

Accelerate and experiment with technology for learning

Motorola University is one of the first corporate universities to bring virtual reality into manufacturing training by using this technology to model complex computer chip fabrication processes. Motorola plans to bring new fabrication plants on line, such as the one planned and under way outside Richmond, Virginia. The fabrication facilities will require new technical-level employees to be trained in these fabrication processes. Motorola's leadership sees virtual reality training playing a major part in a corporate certification program for equipment operators (Corporate Universities International, 1998b, p. 9).

Southern Company College has made strides into interactive satellite distance learning (Younker, 1998). Other useful technologies include computer-based courses; NationsBank Technology Training Group has delivered more than 275 such courses through its virtual campus (Daniel, 1998).

Increase alliances between higher education institutions and corporate universities

"Now larger corporate universities such as Motorola's are forming partnerships with accredited colleges to design degree programs that are more work-related" (Watson, 1995, p. 50), which can be seen in the recent development of a semiconductor technical education degree program by J. Sargeant Reynolds Community College in Richmond, Virginia, to support Motorola's new manufacturing facility. This development supports Burman's contention that business will continue to turn to higher education for partners in training rather than attempt to compete in its milieu.

With regard to alliances between corporate universities and academia, "Corporate partnerships with traditional universities succeed when both parties think carefully about what is expected from each other—and about how to bridge the very real differences in culture between the corporate and academic worlds" (Meister, 1998b, p. 3). Both players have developed increased interest in partnering. The corporate world needs to maximize human potential, given the shortened shelf life of knowledge and the fast-paced technological change. The university needs to move closer to the business community to deliver technically relevant instructional programs. Corporate university programs, in turn, benefit from such partnerships in that corporate students gain university-accredited degrees that are portable.

Increasing numbers of firms are forming close partnerships with traditional colleges so they can offer their employees portable credentials in the form of college degrees. Table 12 presents a cross section of these firms and college partners.

In order to succeed, the partners in corporate-university partnerships and alliances must work together to develop the following:

- A shared mindset about customer service, innovation, and continuous improvement
- Clear expectations for learning objectives and course development
- Flexibility and responsiveness in building the alliance
- Complementary institutional needs and goals
- Ownership rights of intellectual property clearly defined
- Financial and nonfinancial commitments clearly defined
- Adequate infrastructure to explore a partnership
- Commitment to building an open dialogue and continually renewing the partnership with fresh thinking (Meister, 1998b, p. 183–184; Meister, 1998c, p. 38–43)

The U.S. Internal Revenue Service has also moved into the corporate university milieu. Beginning in 1994, the IRS commissioned a corporate university to respond to its personnel education and training needs, with a special emphasis on "inculcating employees with an understanding of a company's values, culture and mission" (Porter, 1997, p. 114).

Academic-corporate alliances require that the participating partners align their institutional goals and objectives. This

TABLE 12

Corporate Universities, Partners, and Programs

Firm	Corporate College	College/University Partner	Major Program
American Express	American Express Quality University	Rio Salado Community College	Customer service A.S.
Bell Atlantic	The NEXT STEP	23-college consortium in New England	Telecommunications technology A.S.
Cigna Corporation	Cigna University	University of Pennsylvania Wharton School of Management	Young broker program
Daimler-Benz	Daimler-Benz University	University of Southern California	Executive development
Lord Corp.	Lord Institute for Technical & Management Training	Erie Co. Technical Institute & NW Pennsylvania Technical Institute	Granted licensure to offer proprietary education to supplier chain
Maryland State Employees Credit Union	SECU University	Community Colleges of Baltimore	Credit union management
Motorola Corporation	Motorola University	J. Sargeant Reynolds Community College and other colleges nationwide	A.S. and certificate programs in semiconductor manufacturing
National Semiconductor	National Semiconductor University	Mission College & San Jose State University	Strategic planning, management education, technical training
Southern Co.	Southern Co. College	Emory University consortium	Global business development
United Healthcare	United Healthcare Learning Institute	Rensselaer Learning Institute	Management and technical training
Whirlpool Corporation	Whirlpool Brandywine Creek Performance Center	Indiana University, University of Michigan	Executive development

alignment must recognize the partnering institutions' con-comitant responsibilities for continually updating workforce education and training. Both institutions must recognize the shortened shelf life of education and their organizations' responsibilities for creating a system to bridge the gaps in education created by changing technology (Cantor, 1997). The college must also have a structure that supports corpo-rate education and an infrastructure that can support just-in-time responses to corporate needs for education and train-ing. This collegiate mindset and infrastructure must include staff that have the authority to develop courses and curricula rapidly in response to a firm's needs. Collegiate and corpo-rate partners must develop a shared vocabulary and sense of trust (Meister, 1998b).

Academic-corporate alliances require that the participat-ing partners align their institutional goals and objectives.

Accreditation

Increasing numbers of corporate universities see a benefit in offering college-accredited courses to their employees. Doing so requires a partnership with a college or university or, alternatively, applying for and meeting the regional accrediting agency's requirements for accreditation of the corporate university itself. Meister (1998b) discusses Lord Corporation's experiences with this process. Lord wished to offer collegiate-level education and training to its supplier chain and to do so initially partnered with Erie County (Pennsylvania) Technical Institute to offer college-level courses. Lord's corporate college, the Lord Institute, was then created through licensure application as a Pennsylvania educational institution. Lord is now able to offer cost-effective education and training and use the rev-enue received to fund its internal training programs. Corporate universities have become regionally chartered to offer a range of college degrees, from associate degrees to master's degrees. The Arthur D. Little Corp. developed the Arthur D. Little School of Management to provide management-level training to its workforce. The School of Management offers a one-year Master of Science in Management plus shorter executive education programs. To achieve its goal, ADL applied for degree-granting status from the commonwealth of Massachusetts. It then applied for and received regional accreditation from the New England Association of Schools and Colleges

(Meister, 1998b, p. 203). ADL has also sought accreditation from the American Association of Collegiate Schools of Business. Inasmuch as AACSB standards require a full-time faculty, ADL has aligned with Babson College, according to Meister, for a joint faculty appointment.

Consortia

Also on the rise are consortia between corporate universities and traditional academies. In such arrangements, as described by Meister (1998b), two or more firms pool their needs for educating and training workers and partner with a college or university to receive services. The arrangement between Southern Company and Emory University is an example. Southern Company needed executive education for employees and perceived that other Atlanta-based firms had similar needs. Guided by this need and vision, Southern Company College led the way for a dozen firms to align through a consortium with Emory University. Emory University delivers a three-week educational program over a four-month period to the employees of the 12 firms. "The consortium membership requires member companies to send at least two participants annually to the programs, each paying a tuition ranging from $9,000 to $11,000 per participant" (Meister, 1998b, p. 199). Similarly, United Healthcare of Minnesota needed cost-effective management and technical training for its workforce. Much of its staff, however, was at remote locations. Having compiled a list of other firms with a similar need, United Healthcare's chief instructional officer set out to find learning partners. Rensselaer Learning Institute (RLI) was selected to deliver management and technical training at a distance via interactive compressed video. RLI also provides United Technologies with similar programs and serves as a broker for other universities, including Boston University, Carnegie Mellon University, Stanford University, and Massachusetts Institute of Technology (Meister, 1998b, p. 200).

The relevant factors for corporate universities to consider in choosing learning partners include (in order of importance) flexibility, responsiveness, a shared vision, proximity, track record, and prestige (Meister, 1998c).

Summary

Much growth and development have taken place in the corporate university movement since Nash & Hawthorne's earlier work. We have witnessed the development of an institution dedicated to formalizing a learning culture in business organizations. This institution is building a bridge to the traditional university for much of its service delivery.

The challenge is to find the common ground necessary to form lasting partnerships of traditional colleges and corporate colleges. The challenge is to identify the quid pro quo—benefits to be derived by both academic and entrepreneur from such cooperation.

DEVELOPING A SUSTAINING MODEL
FOR PARTNERSHIPS

This monograph has reported on the growth and proliferation of higher education delivered outside the academy. It
has described the extent to which corporate America and
other organizations and institutions have entered the
business of providing formal higher and adult education to
their constituents and customers. Business has not gone it
alone to provide education and training to its employees
(C. Taylor, 1999). We have uncovered significant evidence of
business partnering with education to achieve training goals.

These writings have analyzed the manner and extent to
which the traditional academic institution has responded
to this competition and challenge, as well as changes sought
by its changing student body. Having reviewed and highlighted the major findings of the literature, the challenge is
now to pull together a holistic model for delivery of higher
education outside the academy. College and university faculty and leaders must do more than coexist with their respective communities in delivering higher education outside
the academy. The goal must be to meet student constituents'
needs and simultaneously maximize organizational resources
to complement, support, and partner with other organizations also providing education and training. Thus, the
objective in this monograph is to define processes for effective cooperation with other community-based constituents in
providing education and training outside the academy. What
is the long-range impact on the academy of the trends indicated in the literature?

Implications for the Academy

First, more students will embark on higher education with a
definite inclination toward using the computer for learning,
information gathering, and information processing, causing
the traditional academy to accelerate its move into building
an infrastructure capable of supporting computing on and
off campus. This demand on the part of students will cause
faculty to embrace technology as they develop and teach
courses. Increased use of computers in classroom instruction
and development of distance learning courses will accelerate
to meet the demand.

The increased time pressures experienced by students,
who for the most part are older and more mature than their
earlier counterparts, will cause the traditional academy to
adopt more flexible scheduling patterns and practices for

The goal must be to meet student constituents' needs and simultaneously maximize organizational resources to complement, support, and partner with other organizations also providing education and training.

instructional delivery—perhaps compressed semesters, short sessions, and Web-based instructional delivery.

Increasing competition for students is becoming very visible. Competition is a prime motivator of traditional academies to better cooperate and partner with a plethora of organizations to more effectively reach students. This competition will continue to come from entities and organizations not primarily in business or education, such as nonprofit, community-based, and faith-based organizations.

Far more forms of corporate-academic partnerships will take shape. They will include development and delivery of programs by corporate entities with the college, as well as privatization of services within our institutions well beyond the bookstore and food service. We will look for effective means to provide distance learning, virtual textbook delivery, and 24-hour access to college services such as libraries via the Internet.

The academy will embrace the Internet to join in cooperative programming with international academic partners in far greater numbers. Jointly developed and delivered programs will facilitate development of a worldwide workforce and undoubtedly contribute to a better worldwide understanding among its citizens.

We are witnessing an increasingly tight labor market. To help address this situation, colleges and universities must reorganize to better meet needs of the corporate workforce for education and training. This reorganization will include corporate partnerships, new recognition by academic leaders of the value of their cooperative education staffs and program capabilities, and recognition of the value of this market venue to contribute to the overall financial well-being of the institution as a whole. The academy will position itself to serve as the vendor of education and training for corporate universities within firms. Many more firms' corporate universities will reach out to the university to meet their education and training needs as faculties continue to embrace articulation agreements with their corporate partners to recognize industry education and training for college credit.

The traditional academy will pay more attention to ensuring workers' skills and competence as a component of measuring quality in the delivery of academic programs. Part of this drive will come from the increased competition, and part will come from the vocal expressions of business leaders and legislators.

Finally, the traditional academy will recognize the need to provide its students with more opportunities for lifelong education, both professional and avocational.

To meet these challenges, the following programmatic guidance is provided.

Moving Forward: A Model Evolves

As stated earlier, the growth of higher education outside the academy has evolved through and affected three entities: the college or university itself, the corporate or business community, and the community at large. How then can a college or university coexist with others to deliver higher education outside the academy? Meister (1998b) presented a framework for building corporate-college partnerships that can serve as a model for multiple kinds of partnerships. Let's look at what has been learned from a review of the literature about the eight elements that make up that framework as it involves the college or university, the corporate or business community, and the community at large.

- *Identify institutional needs and goals that complement those of business and industry and/or potential corporate and community-based partners.*

Probably the most significant finding of this review of the literature has been the growth and proliferation of private and for-profit institutions of higher education. A plethora of privately held and for-profit ventures offering traditional higher education as well as technical skills and computer-based training has emerged. Levine and Cureton (1998) discussed the notion that "living-learning" communities are quickly disappearing from traditional college campuses as students seek quick approaches to acquiring a higher education. As our student body continues to seek quick-response technical training and Internet-based training, Internet-based higher education is also rapidly growing. In addition, as the market for corporate training has increased, proprietary institutions are continuing to flourish, thus presenting a competitive challenge to traditional colleges and universities.

Therefore, to meet the challenge, traditional colleges should assess their student and community needs and

---

identify whether market niches exist that they can best serve in partnership or independently. For example, a college might identify human resource needs of local businesses that it believes it can meet.

The literature has found that businesses are seeking better relationships with their local colleges. With the growth of education and training delivered by the firm for employees and customers, businesses are finding that investment in employee training pays off in terms of employees' loyalty to the organization and competence in job performance. In fact, institutions such as New York University and Harvard University realize upward of $92 million and $150 million annually, respectively.

A quid pro quo must be mutually understood. Partnerships between colleges and businesses will be sustained only when institutional needs and goals are complementary. These needs and goals must be openly celebrated so that leaders and workers understand them. And when complementary goals do exist, collaboration becomes a must.

Community (or two-year) colleges must recognize that customized corporate training for local business and industry can no longer be considered an activity adjunct to the mission of the college (Gose, 1999). Most community colleges (and a significant number of senior colleges) incorporate design and delivery of training programs for business and industry as an institutional mission. It now represents an opportunity to increase the revenue base of the institution and embellish the college's academic programs and student career opportunities through closer relationships with the business community.

If it is in fact an institutional mission, then the institution must develop the necessary resources. Hence, the institution must have the capacity to handle the kinds of corporate education and training it envisions delivering: a staff person who understands the culture and language of the business world and can analyze and articulate the needs of businesses for education and training; access to instructors (the institution's own or adjunct faculty); curriculum design support; reasonable institutional experience in selected technical disciplines, administrative support, and oversight; and access to laboratories and equipment on and off campus.

Many colleges are beginning delivery of academic programs and instruction via the Internet. Using this method of delivery means ensuring that your college has the electronic infrastructure and faculty development expertise on hand to support these ventures. Support for development and delivery of courses must be made available so that faculty can meet students' and the community's needs.

The literature reveals many well-developed academic-corporate partnerships ranging from the semiconductor industry's SEMATECH to the Cisco Systems' nationwide Networking Academy programs to Microsoft's partnership with the American Association of Community Colleges and member colleges nationwide to Johns Hopkins University's partnership with Caliber Learning Network. The need of the semiconductor manufacturing industry for access to prospective workers and technicians with associate degrees provided the motivation for the industry to form the SEMATECH consortium. SEMATECH assists in partnering semiconductor manufacturing facilities with local community colleges wishing to provide the SEMATECH curriculum. Similarly, the literature reveals that the need of Cisco Systems for access to prospective networking technician workers and the needs of colleges and universities for access to up-to-date equipment and curriculum in computer technologies brought those partners together.

Microsoft's rationale for investing more than $7 million in higher education partnerships was that doing so allowed Microsoft to capitalize on the well-positioned community college to gain access to the nontraditional student, who could be tomorrow's information technology specialist. Microsoft recognizes that community colleges maintain close ties with their local business community and respond quickly to local businesses' needs for workforce training.

Aligning needs and goals is also a highlight of the Johns Hopkins University–Caliber Learning Network partnership. This partnership grew out of a need by JHU to offer its executive graduate certificate in the business of medicine to a wider physician audience. At the time this partnership was started, Caliber, a venture of Sylvan Learning Systems and MCI, sought an academic partner to test its new business of providing technology solutions to educational institutions. Caliber would bring the technology and venture capital; JHU would bring the course content and academic expertise.

In the case of corporate universities, it is again essential to align needs and goals. Motorola chose to begin a corporate university to maintain product quality through a trained and caring workforce. It partnered with selected colleges whose goals were closely aligned with its own. In Virginia, J. Sargeant Reynolds Community College serves firms by providing quality assurance and customer training; Motorola University is one of its partners for such training. The faculty must be involved early on and must understand the relationships with their corporate counterparts in order to feel at ease in sharing certain academic roles and responsibilities with corporate instructors.

- *Establish clear expectations for learning objectives and course development.*

A sound planning process should ensure that educational program goals and objectives are specified and that all partners understand them. In the case of customized corporate training, learning objectives serve as the foundation blocks for the overall partnership. Learning objectives identified for a training course or program should be measurable, and the parties should understand how an assessment process will operate and how changes to program policy will work.

Corporate-college partnerships fail when the academic partner assumes that delivering a college course to a business partner will automatically meet the needs of that firm's employees. The college must stay close to the educational program to ensure that the firm's needs are in fact met. In other words, if either the academic or the business partner believes that some aspect of the program is not operating satisfactorily, a process should be agreed on whereby a needed change can happen without undue pain to the overall program. Roles and responsibilities for effecting needed changes should also be made clear up front.

These facts also hold true in design and delivery of Internet-based and other distance learning media. Education and training programs acquired through a contractual agreement with firms that broker programs, such as Educational Video Conferencing, should also be acquired and evaluated based on learning outcomes that meet the goals of the college's student communities.

As the literature reveals, the quid pro quo for most partnerships is a desire by the business partner to acquire the expertise of the higher education institution in course and curriculum development. In the case of SEMATECH, the semiconductor firms formed a college-industry partnership to promote course and curriculum development for training workers. Microsoft views its participation in the partnership as an opportunity to access college expertise in course development.

Similarly, corporate university projects have as their central focus an access to quality course development from their higher education partners. They also must be predicated on learning objectives. In addition, the ability to fold corporate training into opportunities for a firm's employees to earn a degree becomes an added plus.

- *Clearly define financial and nonfinancial commitments.*
Perhaps the most essential element of any partnership, but especially an academic-business partnership, is the commitment of financial and nonfinancial resources by all parties. A successful partnership demands that such considerations be clearly defined at the program's commencement.

Why? Competition to offer education and training services is becoming keener. Nontraditional nonprofit community-based organizations providing education and training in competition with traditional institutions of higher education are increasing their presence. Such organizations include public television, libraries, hospitals, community centers, and the like. Alternate venues for accessing college-level education are growing as a result of these various forces. Therefore, to ensure that your college or university is actually able to offer financially competitive services that do not adversely affect the institution's fiscal health, an analysis of costs for services must include all indirect costs, such as staff time and overhead for use of rooms. Discuss with partners the costs of services to the public through your joint venture, and determine the competitive price that you would need to choose for the training services. And do not forget the possibilities of sharing corporate staff as faculty. Then determine whether the cost would yield enough revenue to make the venture worthwhile.

Good legal counsel is essential at the start of a new partnership. A clear contract or memorandum of understanding spelling out all financial and operating considerations should

Corporate-college partner-ships fail when the academic partner assumes that delivering a college course to a business partner will automatically meet the needs of that firm's employees.

be drawn up at the commencement of the partnership. Such a contract or memorandum of understanding will need to be revisited as the partnership matures. The contract between Greenville Technical College and Kaplan Learning for student developmental services, for example, defined the relationship between the parties and provided for benchmarking progress and monitoring services.

Corporate training provided by colleges to local business and industry usually operates on a cost-reimbursement basis. That is, the college charges fees for education and training services that are determined based on the cost of instructors and materials, laboratory fees, and the like; possibly an amount for college overhead; and a predetermined profit that the college wishes to realize from its services. An entity venturing into this kind of activity should study the competition in the community from other profit-making and community-based organizations offering similar services, and consider the college's mission to the community, relationships with local business (in terms of existing college fundraising and the college's foundation), and goals of the organization for additional revenues from the corporate training activities.

As for instructional delivery via the Internet, as more colleges align contractually with private providers for on-line courses, clean contractual relationships are also becoming more imperative. Costs for Internet linkage to the college's homepage should be identified. Costs to students for accessing the course materials through the partnering provider must be specified, as well as the monies realized by each party as a result of the venture.

In many cases, the college's nonprofit foundation becomes the medium for entering into a contract with an outside organization or vendor. Organization for administration of partnerships may become important to a college at some point as well. Success requires that issues such as a central point of contact at the college be identified for students and prospective students to access information and counseling services. In addition, e-mail capability has become essential for dispensing information and receiving questions. Plans for record keeping must be made before such a partnership is begun. The Dallas County Community College District, for example, has initiated the Office for Partnerships (Wenrich, 1999).

- *Build a commitment to an open dialogue and continually renew the partnership with fresh thinking.*

Having discussed financial and legal considerations, we now have a basis for open dialogue. Good ideas and working partnerships go hand in hand when an open dialogue and receptiveness to new and refreshing ideas exist. How do colleges keep an open dialogue with their students and industry partners?

Perhaps your institution develops a relationship with a local small firm to provide education and training in computer applications. Having offered courses on site in the firm for a number of semesters, you approach the firm's owner with an idea to recognize some of this employee training as meeting some of the requirements for a college degree for the firm's workers. Colleges have demonstrated a willingness to stay current with their programs through outreach and articulation with business and industry, using such processes as the ACE-CCRS. Developing processes to allow college programming to respond quickly to the needs of business and industry is a must for maintaining open dialogue, as described earlier for the Virginia community colleges.

With the emergence of industry certification programs as a primary area of customer interest, many colleges are seeking opportunities to offer education and training aimed at preparing students for certification exams. Colleges should feel comfortable competing in this arena. Such innovation can become a new area for training and course development in those technology areas for which industries have adopted certification benchmarks. Perhaps consider how noncredit training activities in this area can be integrated with college credit courses to afford employees of participating firms the ability to gain college credits toward eventual degrees as part of their job training.

An increasingly popular way for colleges and universities to help business sectors organize for education and training is through sponsorship and development of industry consortia, often collocated in a geographical cluster. These activities add significantly to the firm's competitive edge in the market. Expansions in corporate training have resulted in new forms of corporate training organizations and partnerships for training and development. A key ingredient of successful ongoing partnerships is putting all parties' concerns on the table. Seek solutions to problems openly and in the best interest of the partnership.

- *Build an alliance through flexibility and responsiveness.*

As we assess college-corporate-community partnerships, we should keep in mind that the traditional student body is changing. As a result of increasing demands on time and financial resources, students are demanding access to college study via the Internet. Students expect instructional services on demand. Moreover, digital technologies have revolutionized society, including the workplace. Hence, another force driving the movement of higher education outside the academy is colleges' and universities' use of computer-based technologies to deliver instruction to their students. Keep abreast of how other colleges use technology to meet students' needs and adopt good ideas. These areas are where we can more fully extend our services to our communities and perhaps garner corporate support in doing so.

A key ingredient of successful ongoing partnerships is putting all parties' concerns on the table.

Thus, a partnership must strive for an attitude of flexibility and responsiveness for it to survive the test of time. It is important to keep in mind that academic institutions and business organizations are very different and do not always share the same goals. Partnerships happen when both concerns see a need to capitalize on each other's expertise. Given this mutual need, both partners must recognize that flexibility in arriving at policies and procedures for the relationship must be maintained, and both partners must strive to be responsive to each other's needs. In the Kaplan–Chattanooga State Technical Community College project, for example, flexibility was absolutely necessary to overcome resistance to change from college staff.

Colleges, especially two-year institutions, are moving toward development of processes to make change easier when it comes to forms of workforce training. Colleges need tools such as the Virginia Community College System's two-year degree model, which permits rapid response to businesses' needs for worker training.

- *Establish an adequate infrastructure to explore a partnership.*

Both the business and the academic partner must have adequate infrastructure to move forward on a concept of partnership. This infrastructure includes adequate financial resources, regulatory structure, personnel, space, ongoing business activities, and organizational configurations. In short, available resources must support good ideas. In many cases, the reason that colleges have chosen to partner with on-line for-profit ventures or to join consortia with other colleges has been to gain access to hardware and programming it does not possess.

As distance learning partnerships become more commonplace, adequate technology infrastructure is becoming more essential. The literature reveals the various institutions that have found a place in this newly emerging market. The University of Phoenix and the Open University of the United States are but two examples of private ventures into the traditional college milieu that capitalize on the new student demographics and technology. As Florida State University has demonstrated, a public-private venture can prove mutually beneficial when both parties maintain an open dialogue.

In the Dallas County Community College District, institutional infrastructure is essential for developing and sustaining viable partnerships. DCCCD suggests that viable partnerships afford the college a chance to better serve its students through penetration into new segments of its community and access to technologies that would otherwise be too expensive. Caliber Learning Network notes that the corporate partner is in the best position to add those infrastructure elements—technology, marketing, and production—that otherwise might be too costly for a college to move forward on a project.

- *Establish a shared mindset about customer service, innovation, and continuous improvement.*

Academic leaders must understand that American businesses will provide lifelong learning to their employees and customers with or without the assistance of colleges or universities. When opportunities to partner with a local business emerge, the academic institution should enter the dialogue with the intention of ensuring that it will partner with business only when both partners share a common vision about customer service (how the targeted student population will be served), innovation (how programs will be designed, developed, and delivered), and continuous improvement (how program outcomes will be evaluated and what will occur with the results of that evaluation). These agreements are essential if a partnership is to succeed.

In many cases, the processes and procedures for conducting a businesslike relationship must be streamlined. Easy procedures for registration at the workplace, direct billing of the firm for tuition, on-line registration, and counseling are but a few of the ways to make the college more user friendly.

Other forms of public-private partnerships have been formed specifically to provide college services. Kaplan Educational Centers is a prime example, offering developmental learning services external to the college. The bottom line, however, is that industry and higher education will join forces when each partner perceives it is fairly treated.

Caliber Learning Network suggests that viable partnerships will develop when all partners understand and value each other's culture and organizational differences. Moreover, such a partnership should ensure that common measures of success and a plan for dealing with the unexpected be developed. Mutual celebration of the project's successes and outcomes is recommended.

The partnership between Dallas County Community College District and Texas Instruments to provide TQM services to TI's suppliers afforded DCCCD an opportunity to serve new customers as well as renew and refresh the college's faculty. DCCCD's partnerships with Middlesex Research Institute, the U.S. Navy, and Harcourt Brace Jovanovich afforded the district's colleges an opportunity to employ faculty to develop telecourses and Internet-based courses. DCCCD views these partnerships as more valuable than just opportunities for generating revenue; it sees them as an opportunity to enhance learning for students.

- *Clearly define ownership rights of intellectual property.*
Along with other items, the memorandum of understanding must define ownership rights of intellectual property for all parties. As we move into more information technology–oriented ventures, these kinds of issues become more pressing. As those colleges and universities that are well ahead of the power curve have experienced with courses offered over the Internet, a clear understanding with faculty and with partnering organizations about course ownership is essential.

Partnerships such as Jones Education or Caliber Learning Network take great care to delineate the ownership of college faculty–developed courses and materials. Certainly, to ensure that the partnership works and that faculty buy into the program, it is essential that faculty realize benefits from such relationships.

Kaplan Learning and Chattanooga State Technical Community College came to such an understanding about the ownership of materials developed as part of their partnership. Faculty use Kaplan staff to consult on course development, and faculty retain ownership of course materials developed for college use. Copyright and ownership is still the one part of public-private partnerships that needs the most attention, according to Caliber Learning Network.

The movement has witnessed a tremendous growth of college-developed training delivered on site to local business and industry. Workforce education at the nation's colleges and universities has increased significantly as our nation's colleges have recognized the market created by business and industry for quality training. Services include technical skills and basic skills, employee readiness services, and English as a second language. Colleges and universities, both public and private, are now entering the market to train workers in order to generate monies to supplement diminishing tax revenues and endowments.

Colleges and universities have developed a number of processes and mechanisms to collaborate beyond the walls of the traditional academy. They include processes and conventions for recognizing corporate education (e.g., ACE-CCRS) as well as processes for recognizing skills acquired during adult life outside the academy (including military training) as fulfilling some of the requirements for a formal college degree. Many colleges offer continuing education units for noncredit education and training courses in order to enable employees to earn increased salaries, renew certifications and licenses, and articulate employer-sponsored training into college degree programs. The issues of accreditation of higher education, quality control of the learning content and environment, the use of technology in learning, ownership of the curriculum, and maintenance of state-of-the-art programs have been addressed in some fashion by both entrepreneurs and higher education institutions.

Copyright and ownership is still the one part of public-private partnerships that needs the most attention.

Among new configurations for business organizations is the corporate university, an institution developed by the corporation to meet changes in business created by a global economy and increased competition. The corporate university is a centralized umbrella for a firm's education and training for its employees and customers (Meister, 1998a). The literature suggests that corporate universities had increased to more than 1,200 by early 2000.

The corporate university has also provided a means for a business and an educational institution to partner, cooperate, and collaborate. It has become the single most strategic mechanism to provide the kind of level ground on which these two differently oriented types of organizations can collaborate to achieve their mutual goals and objectives.

Summary

It is clear from a review of the literature that the future of higher education in America will include significant partnerships and joint ventures with the private sector business community. No longer can academe survive within itself, closed off from the business community. Technology, the demands of students and businesses alike, and the tightening of public budgets have caused this change. Successful colleges and universities of tomorrow will be able to enter into partnerships and joint ventures that maximize their resources and attract the kinds of resources and capabilities from outside that bring new opportunities for the student body and faculty.

REFERENCES

Allen, C. (1996). Corporations grow their own best employees at corporate universities. *Journal of Career Planning & Employment, 56*(2), 24–27, 61–64.

American Society for Training and Development. (1998). How industry views higher education as a partner. *Issues & Trends Report: Industry/Education Partnership Forum.* Alexandria, VA: American Society for Training and Development.

Arenson, K. W. (1998, October 7). N.Y.U. sees profits in virtual classes. *New York Times,* 8.

Aronowitz, S. (1998, March/April). The new corporate university: Higher education becomes higher training. *Dollars & Sense, 216,* 32–35.

Bachler, C. J. (1997a). Corporate universities are catching on. *Workforce, 76*(6), 96.

Bachler, C. J. (1997b). The trainer's role is turning upside down. *Workforce, 76*(6), 93–105.

Bassi, L. J., & Cheney, S. (1997). Benchmarking the best. *Training & Development, 51*(11), 60–64.

Bassi, L. J., Cheney, S., & Lewis, E. (1998, November). Trends in workplace learning: Supply and demand in interesting times. *Training & Development,* 51–77.

Bassi, L. J., Cheney, S., & Van Buren, M. (1997, November). Training industry trends 1997. *Training & Development,* 46–59.

Bassi, L. J., & Van Buren, M. (1998). The 1998 ASTD state of the industry report. *Training & Development, 52*(1), 21–43.

Bassi, L. J., & Van Buren, M. (1999). The 1999 ASTD state of the industry report. *Training & Development Supplement, 53*(1), 1–27.

Beckman, B. M., & Doucette, D. (1993, February). Community college workforce training programs: Expanding the mission to meet critical needs. Battle Creek, MI: League for Innovation in the Community College. (ERIC Document Reproduction Service No. ED 367 425)

Bishop, P. (1996, June). Education and industry links: A tripartite model. *School Science Review, 77*(281), 27–33.

Blumenstyk, G. (1998, April 24). Colleges wonder if Microsoft is their next competitor. *Chronicle of Higher Education,* A33–34.

Blumenstyk, G. (1999a, March 19). In a first, the North Central Association accredits an on-line university. *Chronicle of Higher Education,* A27.

Blumenstyk, G. (1999b, April 9). The marketing intensifies in distance learning. *Chronicle of Higher Education,* A27–28+.

Bosley, D. S. (1995, Fourth Quarter). Collaborative partnerships: Academia and industry working together. *Technical Communication,* 611–619.

Braun, H. W., & Arden, K. (1998). University of Southern California's partnership with Daimler-Benz: Model international corporate/college partnership. *Corporate Universities International, 4*(1), 10.

Cantor, J. A. (1997). Registered pre-apprenticeship: Successful practices linking school to work. *Journal of Industrial Teacher Education, 34*(3), 35–58.

Cantor, J. A. (1998). Semiconductor manufacturing comes to Virginia: Developing partnerships for workforce education and training. *ATEA Journal, 25*(3), 8–9.

Cantor, J. A. (1999, Fall). CISCO systems networking academies and the Virginia Community College System: A model information systems technology training partnership. *ATEA Journal, 27*(2), December 1999–January 2000, 16–18.

Chase, N. (1998). Lessons from the corporate university. *Quality, 37*(6), 120.

Chronicle of Higher Education. (1999, May 7). Harcourt higher education academic deans, bulletin board, advertisement, B35.

Claggett, C. A., & Alexander, H. J. (1995, July). *Maryland community college workforce training evaluation and needs assessment survey.* Baltimore: Maryland Association of Deans and Directors of Continuing Education/Community Services. (ERIC Document Reproduction Service No. ED 384 376)

College Board. (1998, December 2). *The privatization of higher education: Who is the competition?* Public Broadcasting Service Teleconference, Part I. New York: College Board.

College Board. (1999, March 3). *The privatization of higher education: When to compete, how to cooperate.* Public Broadcasting Service Teleconference, Part II. New York: College Board.

Commission on Colleges of the Southern Association of Colleges and Schools. (1988). *The continuing education unit: Criteria and guidelines* (3rd ed.). Atlanta, GA: Commission on Colleges of the Southern Association of Colleges and Schools.

Corporate Universities International. (1998a). 1998 survey of corporate university future directions: Corporate universities transform management education, *4*(1), 4–5.

Corporate Universities International. (1998b). Preliminary findings from the American Council on Education's survey of postsecondary partnerships with business and industry, *4*(1), 9–11.

Daniel, B. (1998). *Virtual tour: NationsBank technology training's virtual campus.* Presentation to the 3rd Annual Symposium and Expo: Corporate Universities Enter the 21st Century, Nashville, TN.

Doucette, D. (1997, February). What will community colleges do when Microsoft and Disney deliver high-quality, accredited higher education and training to the businesses and homes of most Americans? In *Walking the tightrope: The balance between innovation and leadership.* Proceedings of the 6th Annual Conference of the Chair Academy, Reno, NV.

Eurich, N. P. (1990). *The learning industry: Education for adult workers.* Princeton, NJ: Carnegie Foundation for the Advancement of Teaching.

Evelyn, J. (1999, March 22). The workforce development dilemma: Some question whether allowing business to exert influence over curricula sets an unsound precedent. *Community College Week,* 6–7.

Fairweather, J. S. (1990). Education: The forgotten element in industry-university relationships. *Review of Higher Education, 14*(1), 33–45.

Gehrke, R. (1998, October 19). Western Governors University battles accreditation worries. *Community College Week,* 5.

Gjertsen, L. A. (1997, September 29). Cigna U. instructs "future industry leaders." *National Underwriter, 101,* 7–8.

Golfin, P. A., & Curtin, L. A. (1998, March). *Partnerships with community colleges: Vehicles to benefit Navy training and recruiting.* Alexandria, VA: Center for Naval Analyses.

Gose, B. (1999, February 19). Surge in continuing education brings profits for universities: Once regarded as a byproduct, post-baccalaureate programs now provide needed revenues. *Chronicle of Higher Education,* A51–52.

Heide, M. J. (1997, April). The schooling of corporate America: The challenge of worker education programmes. *Industry and Higher Education,* 79–84.

Hoy, J. C. (1998). The skilled worker crunch. *Connection: New England's Journal of Higher Education and Economic Development, 13*(3), 14.

Hunt, T. (1995). *Campus-corporate partnerships: Payoffs and perils.* New Brunswick, NJ: Rutgers University.

Institute for Research on Higher Education, University of Pennsylvania. (1997). Where the dollars are: The market for employers and continuing education. *Change, 29*(2), 39–42.

Itawamba Community College. (1995). *Itawamba Community College and Tecumseh Products Company, Inc.: A high performance work force development partnership.* Tupelo, MS: Itawamba Community College. (ERIC Document Reproduction Service No. ED 380 165)

Klor deAlva, J. (in College Board, December 1998). Presentation during *The privatization of higher education: Who is the competition?* Public Broadcasting Service Teleconference, Part I. New York: College Board.

Kurschner, D. (1997). Getting credit. *Training, 34*(6), 52–54.

Learning organizations: Those who can, teach. (1995, October 28). *The Economist, 337*(7938), 79.

Levine, A. (in College Board, December 1998). Presentation during *The privatization of higher education: Who is the competition?* Public Broadcasting Service Teleconference, Part I. New York: College Board.

Levine, A., & Cureton, J. S. (1998). In *When hope and fear collide: A portrait of today's college student* (pp. 2–14). New York: College Board.

Lively, K., & Blumenstyk, G. (1999, January 29). Sylvan Learning Systems to start a network of for-profit universities overseas. *Chronicle of Higher Education,* A43–44.

Magotte, E. (in College Board, March 1999). Presentation during *The privatization of higher education: When to compete, how to cooperate.* Public Broadcasting Service Teleconference, Part II. New York: College Board.

Mailliard, K. (1997). Sprint: Retention via training. *HR Focus, 74*(10), 84.

McCandless, G. (1998, October). Info technology spawns massive new training market. *Community College Week,* 6+.

Meighan, J. E. (1995, February). *Creative partnership structures: Innovative ways to link colleges and employers.* Paper presented at Workforce 2000, the 3rd annual conference on workforce training of the League for Innovation in the Community College, San Diego, CA. (ERIC Document Reproduction Service No. ED 380 170)

Meister, J. (1998a). Corporate universities and academia develop innovative alliances. *Corporate Universities International, 4*(1), 3–4.

Meister, J. (1998b). *Corporate universities: Lessons in building a world-class work force.* New York: McGraw-Hill.

Meister, J. (1998c, November). Ten steps to creating a corporate university. *Training & Development,* 38–43.

Moore, T. E. (1997). The corporate university: Transforming management education. *Accounting Horizons, 11*(1), 77.

Nash, N. S., & Hawthorne, E. M. (1987). *Formal recognition of employer-sponsored instruction: Conflict and collegiality in postsecondary education.* ASHE-ERIC Higher Education Report No. 3. Washington, DC: Association for the Study of Higher Education.

National Alliance of Business. (1997). Company training and education: Who does it, who gets it and does it pay off? *Workforce Economics, 3*(2), 3–7.

National Coalition of Advanced Technology Centers. (1992). *National coalition of advanced technology centers: Proposal to the nation.* Waco, TX: National Coalition of Advanced Technology Centers. (ERIC Document Reproduction Service No. ED 357 781)

Nimtz, L. E., Coscarelli, W. C., & Blair, D. (1995). University-industry partnerships: Meeting the challenge with a high-tech partner. *SRA Journal/Features, 27*(2), 9–17.

Northeast Utilities System. (1998, Fall). Piecing together the work force development puzzle: Part 2. In *New England development: Policy issues shaping the regional economy.* Hartford CT: Northeast Utilities System.

Ouellette, T. (1998). Corporate training programs go to college. *Computerworld, 32*(15), 20.

Patterson, V. (1996). Industry and education collaborate to shape future workers. *Journal of Career Planning & Employment, 56*(2), 28–32.

Perez, S. A., & Copenhaver, C. C. (1998). Certificates on center stage: Occupational education for a working economy. *Leadership Abstracts, 11*(3), 1–2.

Porter, J. A. (1997, February). Education and training in the IRS today. *The Tax Advisor,* 114–115.

Price, L., et al. (1995, November). *Workforce development and preparation initiatives: Implications for the California community colleges.* Sacramento: California Community Colleges, Academic Senate. (ERIC Document Reproduction Service No. ED 395 623)

Rosa, J. (1998, June 15). Microsoft pays tribute to best and brightest solutions. *Computer Reseller News, 794,* 50.

Rosen, S. (in College Board, December 1998). Presentation during *The privatization of higher education: When to compete, how to cooperate.* Public Broadcasting Service Teleconference, Part I. New York: College Board.

Sammarco, B. (1997). Career courses. *Credit Union Management, 20*(2), 33–34.

Santamaria, T. (1998, April 26). Academic-industry partnerships target IT worker shortage. *Washington Post.*

Selingo, J. (1999a, March 26). Pennsylvania surprises colleges by letting U. of Phoenix open campuses in state. *Chronicle of Higher Education,* A43.

Selingo, J. (1999b, March 12). Technical colleges at a crossroads: As states push for expanded academic programs, are they abandoning hands-on training? *Chronicle of Higher Education,* A28–30.

Skilbeck, M., & Connell, H. (1996). Industry-university partnerships in the curriculum: Trends and developments in OECD countries. *Industry and Higher Education, 11*(1) 9–22.

Slaughter, S. (1998). Federal policy and supply-side institutional resource allocation at public universities. *Review of Higher Education, 21*(3), 209–244.

Stamps, D. (1998, August). The for-profit future of higher education. *Training,* 23–30.

Sullivan, C. (1998). Exciting trends in corporate education and training. *Hawthorne Associates Release.* (On-line: www.Hawthorne-assoc.com)

Sunoo, B. P. (1998). Corporate universities: More and better. *Workforce, 77*(5), 16–17.

Taylor, C. A. (1999, April 19). Putting business in the driver's seat. *Community College Week,* 4.

Taylor, R. L. (in College Board, December 1998). DeVry: Growing a new kind of university. Presentation during *The privatization of higher education: Who is the competition?* Public Broadcasting Service Teleconference, Part I. New York: College Board.

Watson, B. S. (1995). The new training edge: Training has become a way of bonding with employees, and the corporate university is fast becoming the model of choice. *Management Review, 84*(5), 49–51.

Wenrich, W. (in College Board, March 1999). Presentation during *The privatization of higher education: When to compete, how to cooperate.* Public Broadcasting Service Teleconference, Part II. New York: College Board.

Yates, E. L. (1999, March 22). North Carolina's industrial strength: From garment manufacturers to yacht builders, companies flock to a state where workforce training is considered the best in the nation. *Community College Week,* 8–9.

Younker, R. J. (1998). *Interactive distance learning at Southern Company.* Presentation to the 3rd Annual Symposium & Expo: Corporate Universities Enter the 21st Century, Nashville, TN.

INDEX

A

Academia. *See* Higher education

Academia-business partnership. *See* Higher education–business partnerships

Accreditation: corporate college, 62–63; issues of, 32, 33, 51–52

Accreditation Council for Continuing Medical Education, 50

Accrediting Commission for Senior Colleges and Universities, Western Association of Schools and Colleges, 33

Accrediting Commission of Career Schools and Colleges of Technology, 51–52

Accrediting Council of Independent Schools and Colleges, 52

ACE-CCRS, 73

Adult education outreach, 50–51

Advanced Manufacturing Center (Itawamba Community College), 47

Alexander, H. J., 21

Allen, C., 18, 55, 57

American Bankers Association, 47

American Council on Education (ACE), 47–48, 49

American Psychological Association, 33

American Red Cross, 1

American Society for Training and Development (ASTD), 6, 9, 14

Anne Arundel Community College, 50

Apollo Group (University of Phoenix), 30

Arden, K., 43, 58

Area Networking Academy (Cisco), 44–45

Arenson, K. W., 8

Army/ACE Registry Transcript System, 49

Aronowitz, S., 5, 10, 43

Arthur D. Little Corp., 62–63

ASTD survey (1998), 7, 15, 21, 24

AT&T, 47

AT&T Learning Network Virtual Academy, 37

B

Bachler, C. J., 12, 53

Bassi, L. J., 6, 7, 12, 13, 15, 16, 17, 19, 21, 22, 23, 24, 25

Beckman, B. M., 22

Bishop, P., 43

BLS (U.S. Bureau of Labor Statistics), 14

Blue Ridge Community College, 38

Blumenstyk, G., 31, 33, 34, 39, 40

Bosley, D. S., 14

Boston University, 63

Braun, H. W., 43, 58

Business sector: cost of training by, 6–7, 13–15, 16*t*; human research development by, 5–6; interest in education by, 4; learning

---

Higher Education Outside of the Academy

organizations of, 12; partnerships with higher education by, 9–10; training expenditures, by industry, 19*t*. *See also* Higher education–business partnerships

C

Caliber Learning Network, 31, 34–35, 69–70, 75, 76, 77
California State University System, 32, 48
Cantor, J. A., 15, 19, 43, 45, 62
Carnegie Mellon University, 63
Center for Adult Learning and Educational Credentials (ACE), 47
Charles Stuart University, 35
Charter Oak State College, 11, 38, 51
Chase, N., 53
Chattanooga State Technical Community College, 39
Cheney, S., 12, 13, 17
Chronicle of Higher Education, 31
Cisco Certified Internetworking Engineer (CCIE), 45
Cisco Certified Networking Professional (CCNP), 45
Cisco Systems Certified Network Associates (CCNA), 4, 44–45
Cisco Systems Academic Partners, 10, 43, 69
Claggett, C. A., 21
College Credit Recommendation Service (CCRS) (ACE), 47–48
Commission on Higher Education, Middle States Association of Colleges and Schools, 50
Commission on Institutions of Higher Education, North Central Association of Colleges and Schools, 33
Commission on Technical and Career Institutions, New England Association of Schools and Colleges, 52
Connected Education, 35
Continuing education: adult education outreach, 50–51; growth of, 13–14; higher education–industry partnerships and, 46–47; medical, 11–12, 34–35, 50; *See also* Distance learning
Continuing education units (CEUs), 51
Continuous quality improvement (CQI)/TQM training, 15
Copenhaver, C. C., 9
Corporate colleges: accreditation of, 62–63; budget management of, 56–57; corporate management support of, 58–59; growth of, 78; increasing alliance with higher education and, 59–60; by industry sector, 54*t*; learning technology used by, 59; listing of, 61*t*; overview of, 53–55; profit-making opportunities of, 55–56; rise of consortia between academies and, 63; varied learning opportunities/methodologies of, 58. *See also* Higher education–business partnerships; Human resource development
Corporate training expenditures, 16*t*
Corporate Universities International, 55, 59
Corporation for Public Broadcasting, 1, 11, 49
Council for Accreditation of Counseling and Related Educational Programs, 33

Credit by Examination Program (ACE), 47
Cureton, J. S., 8, 29, 30, 67
Curtin, L. A., 11, 49

D
Dabney S. Lancaster Community College, 38
Daimler-Benz Corp., 58
Dallas County Community College District (DCCCD), 73, 75, 76
DANA Corporation, 47
DANTES, 11
Degree versus industry certification, 4–5
Development Dimensions International, 15
DeVry Institutes, 1, 8, 31, 32, 33, 38, 51
Distance learning: development of, 33–34; ownership of curriculum issues of, 34–38; partnerships listed, 36t. *See also* Continuing education
Doucette, D., 22, 46
Drexel University, 34

E
Educational Resources Information Center, 3
Educational Video Conferencing, 34, 70–71
Emory University, 63
Empire State College, 38
Employer-sponsored training. *See* Human resource development/training
Encarta Virtual Globe, 40
Erie County Technical Institute, 55, 62
Eurich, N. P., 13, 49
Evelyn, J., 7, 14, 20

F
Fairweather, J. S., 2
Fielding Institute, 33
FIRE (finance, insurance, and real estate) sector, 15, 18, 54t
Florida State University, 31, 32, 75
Ford's Fairlane Training and Development Center, 57
Forum Corporation, 15

G
Gehrke, R., 32
George Washington University, 37
Gjertsen, L. A., 53, 54
Going the Distance project (public television), 49–50
Golfin, P. A., 11, 49
Gose, B., 14, 23, 68
Greenville Technical College, 39, 72

H

I

higher education, 8–9; impact on training, 7–8; types of learning and, 25*t*

Institute for Research on Higher Education, University of Pennsylvania, 18

Intellectual property ownership, 76–78

Internet: courses given over the, 8–9; financial commitment of using the, 72–73; higher education privatization and the, 33–34; training delivery through the, 24–25

Itawamba Community College, 46

ITT Technical Institutes, 1, 38, 51, 52

J

J. Sargeant Reynolds Community College, 59, 70

Johns Hopkins University, 31, 34–35, 69

Johns Hopkins University–Caliber Learning Network partnership, 31, 34–35, 69–70, 75, 76, 77

Jones Education Company, 37, 40, 77

K

Kaplan Educational Services, 39, 76

Kaplan Learning Centers, 1, 72

Kaplan–Chattanooga State Technical Community College project, 74

Klor deAlva, J., 8, 30, 32

Kurschner, D., 11, 48

L

"Learning Organizations," 17

Learning technologies, 25*t*

Learning Ventures, 34

Levine, A., 8, 29, 30, 67

Lewis, E., 13, 17

Lively, K., 31

Lord Institute, 55, 62

M

Macomb Community College, 46

Magotte, E., 34, 35

Mailliard, K., 57, 58

Maricopa Community College, 43

Massachusetts Bay Community College, 46

Massachusetts Institute of Technology, 63

McCandless, G., 8

MCSE (Microsoft Certified Systems Engineer), 4

Medical education, 11–12, 34–35, 50

Meighan, J. E., 47

Meister, J., 5, 9, 10, 11, 53, 56, 60, 62, 63, 67, 78

Microsoft, 10, 39, 40

Microsoft Certified Systems Engineer computer training, 39

PBS (public television), 50
Pennsylvania Department of Education, 55
Perez, S. A., 9
Pikes Peak Community College, 46
Polytechnic University, 35
Porter, J. A., 60
Price, L., 24
PRIMEDIA Corporate University Network, 35, 37
Productivity Point International, 48
Public access and television, 49–50
Public Broadcasting Service Online, 49

Q
Quality Dynamics survey, 10

R
Regents College, 50
Regional Networking Academy faculty (Cisco Systems), 44
Rensselaer Learning Institute (RLI), 63
Rio Hondo College, 9
Rosa, J., 45
Rosen, S., 39
Route 128–Boston information technology cluster, 19

S
Sammarco, B., 10
Saratoga Institute, 15
Selingo, J., 32
SEMATECH, 19, 43–44, 69, 71
Slaughter, S., 3
Slavenski, 12
Southern Association of Colleges and Schools (SACS), 51
Southern Company College, 57, 59, 63
Stamps, D., 8
Stanford University, 63
State University of New York System, 50
Students: impact of academic-business partnership for, 65–66; no frills service approach demanded by, 29–30; outside the academy interest by, 4
Sullivan, C., 58
Sunoo, B. P., 53
Sylvan Learning Systems, 31, 69

T
Taylor, C., 13
Taylor, R., 32
TCPU (transportation, communications, and public utilities sector), 15, 18, 54*t*

Technology. *See* Information technology
Technology-oriented programs, 38–39
Tecumseh Products Company, 46–47
Thomas Edison State College, 38
Times-Mirror Training Group, 15
Total quality management (TQM), 15
Training & Development's "1998 ASTD State of the Industry
    Report," 7, 15, 21, 24
Training programs. *See* Human resource development/training

U
UCLA Extension, 37
United HealthCare of Minnesota, 63
University of Lincolnshire & Humberside, 35
University of Madrid, 31
University of Maryland University College, 51
University of Pennsylvania, Wharton School of Business, 31
University of Phoenix (UOP), 8, 30, 32, 33, 51, 75
University of Rochester Medical Center, 50
U.S. Bureau of Labor Statistics (BLS), 14
U.S. Department of Labor, 15, 20
U.S. Internal Revenue Service, 60
U.S. military, 49
U.S. Navy, 49, 76

V
Valencia Community College, 46
Van Buren, M., 6, 7, 12, 13, 15, 16, 17, 19, 21, 22, 23, 24, 25
Virginia Community College System, 10–11, 74–75
"Virtual" colleges, 9

W
Watson, B. S., 5, 6, 56, 59
Wenrich, W., 14
Western Association of Schools and Colleges, 32
Wharton School of Business, University of Pennsylvania, 31

X
Xerox Corporation, 47

Y
Yates, E. L., 45
Younker, R. J., 59

The mission of the Educational Resources Information Center (ERIC) system is to improve American education by increasing and facilitating the use of educational research and information on practice in the activities of learning, teaching, educational decision making, and research, wherever and whenever these activities take place.

Since 1983, the ASHE-ERIC Higher Education Report series has been published in cooperation with the Association for the Study of Higher Education (ASHE). Starting in 2000, the series is published by Jossey-Bass in conjunction with the ERIC Clearinghouse on Higher Education.

Each monograph is the definitive analysis of a tough higher education problem, based on thorough research of pertinent literature and institutional experiences. Topics are identified by a national survey. Noted practitioners and scholars are then commissioned to write the reports, with experts providing critical reviews of each manuscript before publication.

Eight monographs (10 before 1985) in the ASHE-ERIC Higher Education Report series are published each year and are available on individual and subscription bases. To order, use the order form on the last page of this book.

Qualified persons interested in writing a monograph for the ASHE-ERIC Higher Education Report series are invited to submit a proposal to the National Advisory Board. As the preeminent literature review and issue analysis series in higher education, the Higher Education Reports are guaranteed wide dissemination and provide national exposure for accepted candidates. Execution of a monograph requires at least a minimal familiarity with the ERIC database, including *Resources in Education* and the current *Index to Journals in Education.* The objective of these reports is to bridge conventional wisdom and practical research.

ADVISORY BOARD

Susan Frost
Office of Institutional Planning and Research
Emory University

Kenneth Feldman
SUNY at Stony Brook

Anna Ortiz
Michigan State University

James Fairweather
Michigan State University

Lori White
Stanford University

Esther E. Gottlieb
West Virginia University

Carol Colbeck
Pennsylvania State University

Jeni Hart
University of Arizona

CONSULTING EDITORS AND REVIEW PANELISTS

William Blank
University of South Florida

Tim Gallineau
Buffalo State College

Joanna D. Hanks
J. Sargeant Reynolds Community College

James C. Hearn
University of Minnesota

Roger Kaufman
Florida State University

Mantha V. Mehallis
Florida Atlantic University

John A. Muffo
Virginia Tech University

Janet J. Palmer
Lehman College

John M. Ritz
Old Dominion University

David Webster
Oklahoma State University

RECENT TITLES

Volume 27 ASHE-ERIC Higher Education Reports

1. The Art and Science of Classroom Assessment: The Missing Part of Pedagogy
   Susan M. Brookhart

2. Due Process and Higher Education: A Systemic Approach to Fair Decision Making
   Ed Stevens

3. Grading Students' Classroom Writing: Issues and Strategies
   Bruce W. Speck

4. Posttenure Faculty Development: Building a System for Faculty Improvement and Appreciation
   Jeffrey W. Alstete

5. Digital Dilemma: Issues of Access, Cost, and Quality in Media-Enhanced and Distance Education
   Gerald C. Van Dusen

6. Women and Minority Faculty in the Academic Workplace: Recruitment, Retention, and Academic Culture
   Adalberto Aguirre, Jr.

Volume 26 ASHE-ERIC Higher Education Reports

1. Faculty Workload Studies: Perspectives, Needs, and Future Directions
   Katrina A. Meyer

2. Assessing Faculty Publication Productivity: Issues of Equity
   Elizabeth G. Creamer

3. Proclaiming and Sustaining Excellence: Assessment as a Faculty Role
   Karen Maitland Schilling and Karl L. Schilling

4. Creating Learning Centered Classrooms: What Does Learning Theory Have to Say?
   Frances K. Stage, Patricia A. Muller, Jillian Kinzie, and Ada Simmons

5. The Academic Administrator and the Law: What Every Dean and Department Chair Needs to Know
   J. Douglas Toma and Richard L. Palm

6. The Powerful Potential of Learning Communities: Improving Education for the Future
   Oscar T. Lenning and Larry H. Ebbers

7. Enrollment Management for the 21st Century: Institutional Goals, Accountability, and Fiscal Responsibility
   Garlene Penn

8. Enacting Diverse Learning Environments: Improving the Climate for Racial/Ethnic Diversity in Higher Education
   Sylvia Hurtado, Jeffrey Milem, Alma Clayton-Pedersen, and Walter Allen

---

Back Issue/Subscription Order Form

Copy or detach and send to:
Jossey-Bass, 350 Sansome Street, San Francisco CA 94104-1342

Call or fax toll free!
Phone 888-378-2537 6AM-5PM PST; Fax 800-605-2665

Individual reports:	Please send me the following reports at $24 each
	(Important: please include series initials and issue number, such as AEHE 27:1)

1. AEHE _____

_____

_____

$ _____ Total for individual reports

$ _____ Shipping charges (for individual reports *only;* subscriptions are exempt from shipping charges): Up to $30, add $5^{50} • $30^{01}–$50, add $6^{50} $50^{01}–$75, add $8 • $75^{01}–$100, add $10 • $100^{01}–$150, add $12 Over $150, call for shipping charge

Subscriptions   Please ❑ start ❑ renew my subscription to *ASHE-ERIC Higher Education Reports* for the year <u>2000</u> at the following rate (8 issues):   U.S.: $144   Canada: $169   All others: $174

Please ❑ start my subscription to *ASHE-ERIC Higher Education Reports* for the year <u>2001</u> at the following rate (6 issues): U.S.: $108   Canada: $133   All others: $138

NOTE: Subscriptions are for the calendar year only. Subscriptions begin with Report 1 of the year indicated above.

$ _____ Total individual reports and subscriptions (Add appropriate sales tax for your state for individual reports. No sales tax on U.S. subscriptions. Canadian residents, add GST for subscriptions and individual reports.)

❑ Payment enclosed (U.S. check or money order only)

❑ VISA, MC, AmEx, Discover Card # _____ Exp. date _____

Signature _____ Day phone _____

❑ Bill me (U.S. institutional orders only. Purchase order required.)

Purchase order #_____

Federal Tax ID 135593032   GST 89102-8052

Name _____

Address _____

_____

Phone_____ E-mail _____

For more information about Jossey-Bass, visit our Web site at:
www.josseybass.com   **PRIORITY CODE = ND1**